17.95

D0394285

WITHDRAWN

Everyday Life
of the
Maya

Mayan bas-relief: a ball player and his defeated opponent.

RALPH WHITLOCK

Everyday Life of
THE MAYA

Drawings by Eva Wilson

Text copyright © Ralph Whitlock 1976
1987 Dorset Press

DORSET PRESS
New York

First published by B.T. Batsford 1976

This edition published by Dorset Press,
a division of Marboro Books Corporation,
by arrangement with B.T. Batsford Ltd.
1987 Dorset Press

ISBN 0-88029-144-3

Printed in the United States of America
M 9 8 7 6 5

CONTENTS

Acknowledgment

The Author and Publishers would like to thank the following for their kind permission to reproduce copyright illustrations: Ferdinand Anton for the *frontispiece*, and for figs 4, 8, 14, 17, 20, 24, 28, 31-2, 34-5, 43, 49-51, 53, 55-6, 59-60, 62-3, 66, 70-2, 75, 77-9, 81-3, 84 (*right*), 85, 89, 91-2; Janet March-Penney for figs 1, 46; Camera Press for figs 3, 10, 11, 13, 21, 48, 73, 80, 94; A. G. Formenti and the Mexican National Tourist Bureau for figs 9, 84 (*left*); J. Allan Cash for figs 12, 86-8, 90; the Mansell Collection for figs 15, 54, 93; the Trustees of the British Museum for figs 57, 96; University Museum, Philadelphia, for fig. 74.

The Illustrations

Everyday Life
of the
Maya

Introduction

When, in Europe, the Roman Empire was plunging into the abyss of the Dark Ages, its great cities devastated and plundered by barbarian hordes from the steppes of Asia, a magnificent civilization was evolving in the forests and jungles of Central America. It grew, like other civilizations, from a humble village culture, creating in due course splendid cities equal in grandeur to almost anything in the Old World. Then, for reasons unknown, it declined and disintegrated. As far as we know, no European eye ever saw it at the height of its glory.

The jungles of Yucatan, Guatemala, Belize and Honduras are peppered with the sacred sites of the Maya. Many a time, in a jungle clearing, I have seen an isolated conical hill, a hundred feet or more in height, covered with dense bushes and tall trees. It looked natural but was not. It was an unexcavated Maya pyramid, of which there are hundreds yet to be investigated.

The idea that Cortes, Pizarro and the other Spanish conquistadores were a gang of bigoted wreckers, ruthlessly destroying civilizations that were beyond their own powers of comprehension, is a popular one. To whatever degree that interpretation is true in Peru and Mexico, it does not apply to the Maya. Their civilization had passed its zenith centuries before the Spaniards arrived.

The city of Mayapan, which controlled the last of the great Maya states, was sacked in what appears to have been a form of civil war in the year AD 1441. Details of the conflict were still remembered when the first Spaniards appeared in Yucatan at the beginning of the next century. Mayapan itself was, however, no more than a rather shoddy replica of the splendid cities which

1 *A thatched hut in a Mayan village in Yucatan, similar in almost every respect to those built by Mayan peasants in Classical times. The thatch was made from palm fronds.*

dominated the Maya people at an earlier period.

In all civilizations there is a tendency towards fragmentation. An empire or federation of nations can be held together for a few centuries by strong rulers, backed by an efficient administration and a loyal army, but disruptive forces are nearly always at work. Let the central power weaken, and the state starts to split into its constituent parts. Each unit clamours for independence and the right to live its own life according to its own laws and customs. We can observe this in country after country in our own age. In the Maya world we see its ultimate result. The once powerful Maya state has entirely disintegrated into a galaxy of peasant communities, each ingrowing and introspective. For them the story of the Tower of Babel would be an uncomfortably accurate parable. The cohesive force which held them together while they built their colossal architectural masterpieces has been lost.

Although their civilization has become a casualty of time, the Maya people themselves are by no means extinct. There are, in fact, more than two million of them living in Central America today. Most are in Belize, Guatemala and the Yucatan peninsula of Mexico, but some are also to be found in the neighbouring republics.

The Maya people tend to be aloof, having little cause to be

2 *The jungles of Central America are studded with what appear to be natural hills but are in fact Mayan pyramids, now overgrown with bushes and trees.*

grateful to the new civilization which has grown up around them. Like other nations of American Indians, they have tried to combat the European aggression which began with Columbus by withdrawing into a private, introspective world of their own. In Belize they occupy inland villages among the hills, the towns and coastal regions being inhabited mainly by the descendants of West Indian negroes who came, in the eighteenth and nineteenth centuries, to work in the forests and plantations. These, with the Latin Americans, make up the three-race population characteristic of all the Central American countries which have a Caribbean seaboard.

In general, the Indians have as little as possible to do with the bustling communities of the coast. When needing cash, they will go to work on a plantation until they have earned just as much money as they require. Then they will down tools and evaporate back to their villages. Many are now nominally Catholic, though their Christianity is of a hybrid type which embodies a mass of traditional beliefs and superstitions. Among those who have been influenced by Protestant missionaries, strange new cults have sprung up in recent years. Characteristic features are an obsession with the impending end of the world, and a strong anti-foreign sentiment—'foreign' meaning anyone who is not an

Indian. Yet once their reserve has been penetrated, they are revealed as a friendly, likeable people.

When I stayed in an Indian village, my hosts took me to see their farm. We plunged into the jungle, which thereabouts was not only dense but precipitous. We clambered up what appeared to be goat tracks, slithered down the opposite slopes, splashed through bogs and crossed streams by balancing precariously on fallen tree-trunks which wobbled underfoot. The overwhelming green jungle closed in over our heads, submerging our paths in perpetual twilight. Magnificent *Morpho* and *Entheus* butterflies danced in the occasional shafts of sunlight. Hummingbirds darted from flower to vivid flower. Toucans flapped around noisily. Exquisite orchids taunted us from their inaccessible perches. We could hear unknown creatures, probably birds or animals but possibly snakes, in the undergrowth. Flies pursued us relentlessly, and we had to take pains to avoid columns of marching ants. Occasionally our guide had, with his machete, to cut great, pendulous lianas which had tangled across the path. From time to time in the emerald twilight we met women, staggering under loads of plantains.

The farmland which we had trekked so far to see was merely an ill-defined plot, hacked out of the jungle: a hillside which looked as if it had been blasted by lightning. The larger tree-trunks still stuck up, like fangs, from the burnt earth. Around them were tangles of half-consumed branches and mounds of debris. In the desolation stood green standards of maize, sparsely distributed and in no regular ranks or order. Around the shabby clearing the giant trees towered menacingly, as though ready to pounce on the alien colony and regain the territory for its own. Which is exactly what would happen, in a year or two's time.

The Indians were practising typical slash-and-burn culti-vation, common throughout the tropics. After the rough clear-ance work, two crops are taken, and then the land is allowed to revert to jungle. The principle is sound enough. It allows the soil to replenish its stores of fertility and prevents leaching and erosion.

In many tropical countries a period of four years elapses before the scrub is cleared and the land used again. In others, the rest period is seven or eight years. These Indians had pushed it to fifteen years, and they stuck to it rigidly. It was evidently a practice which arose when they were living in a more spacious

3 *Mayan women carrying their weekly shopping along the road.*

countryside, with plenty of land available around their village. Now, fleeing before 'civilization', they had retreated to a narrow, rugged peninsula where the system had serious disadvantages. They were forced to trudge farther and farther afield, over mountains and chasms, in order to find usable land: This loyalty to custom bore more heavily on the women than on the men. By a traditional division of labour, the men were responsible for clearing the land, but the women for the cultivation. And included among the women's duties was carrying the produce back to the village!

Was this a typical Maya village? The question cannot really be answered. We might equally as well ask: What is a typical Indo–European village? For the Maya are in many respects as diverse as are Indo–Europeans. There are a dozen or two Mayan languages, which some authorities claim are as different from each other as English is from Swedish or German, while others

5

maintain that they are as nearly allied as are the provincial dialects of Italy or of Spain. Yet when we attempt to define the Maya, we are driven back to the common bond of language. There *is* a Mayan group of languages which presumably derive from one source. They are spoken by Indian tribes who share a common cultural heritage but who are, in physical appearance, scarcely distinguishable from other American Indians. These tribes occupy a fairly well defined area of Central America where their ancestors developed a remarkable civilization. But this is about as far as it is possible to go in defining who a Maya is. From murals and statues it appears that the classical Maya, like their modern descendants, were rather small people, with the average height of a man being about five feet. Their only other distinctive characteristic was their short, broad skulls (which, as we shall note in a later chapter, were often artificially deformed).

The ancestors of the Maya in Central America have been traced back to about 3000 B.C. Their switch from a purely nomadic life to the cultivation of maize and other crops began about 1000 B.C. Five hundred years later they began building in stone. The earliest date recorded in their inscriptions is 31 B.C. (and about this there is still some controversy). Their first great building period started in A.D. 320. A magnificent civilization developed, though with some remarkable and puzzling fluctuations, in the succeeding centuries, till its final eclipse at the fall of Mayapan in 1441. The finest peaks of Mayan achievement belong to the periods A.D. 435–850 and 987–1007.

Our knowledge of the Mayan past is derived largely from architecture and artefacts. Although the Maya evolved a system of writing and produced quite a voluminous literature, Bishop de Landa, one of the first Spanish prelates to rule in those parts, burned most of their books, and only three have survived. There are also numerous inscriptions in stone, but the key to the written language has been lost and at present only about a third of the characters can be deciphered.

Among the characters that we do understand, however, are many concerned with dates. The Maya developed a remarkably accurate calendar, or, to be precise, three interlocking calendars, which they used to predict eclipses of the sun and moon. They were able to calculate that the planet Venus took 584 days to complete its apparent circuit of the heavens; modern astronomers have measured it as 583·92 days. The Maya's calculation of the lunar month was 29·53020 days; ours is 29·53059 days.

To make such accurate calculations the Maya worked out a system of numbers much superior to anything in ancient Europe or Asia, including Greece and Rome. It was a simple system of

4 *Vast areas of Maya ruins have still to be excavated. These imposing remains are at Tikal, one of the great Mayan cities of Yucatan.*

bars and dots, in which they multiplied values by moving the position of a number in a row, just as we do. For instance, we multiply ten by ten by writing 'io', moving the figures one row to the left and then adding a nought, thus 'ioo'. The Maya did much the same thing, except that they worked in vertical columns and multiplied in twenties instead of in tens. They even had a symbol for zero, which is more than had either the Greeks or the Romans.

The intense interest of the Maya in mathematics and the calendar was a result of their obsession with astrology. They tried to predict the future from the movement of the stars, and based their religion on this. Their mathematicians and astronomers were also priests, the organizers of their religion. The Mayan pyramids, too, had a religious significance. As a rule, a new one had to be built every 52 years. Where the same site was chosen the pyramid was simply built around an existing one, which thus increased in size and girth. Excavating a Maya pyramid is rather like peeling the layers of an onion.

Around the pyramids are the buildings occupied by the priests and the palaces of the nobles. The architecture is massive but splendid. Many of the buildings are highly decorated with paintings and sculptures, often in the form of friezes. Maya sculpture tends to be square and chunky, and, as the artists hated an empty space, it is filled with detail almost to the point of confusion. The wall paintings are magnificent and reminiscent in many respects of those of ancient Egypt and India, except that the human figures are more lifelike.

In Yucatan most of the Maya cities are situated near natural waterholes, or *cenotes*, which are of vital importance in that near-waterless country. Some of these waterholes were considered sacred, and over the centuries many gifts were thrown into them. Archaeologists are nowadays salvaging these gifts and from them have learned a great deal about the Mayan civilization. The sacrifices include masterpieces in gold and copper, and also jade which the Maya prized most of all.

As we can read so little of their writing, much of the history of the Maya is still shrouded in mystery. In particular, we do not know why the splendid cities were, one after another, quickly abandoned. The vast ruins still arouse in us the same sense of awe and wonder that filled the Spanish conquistadores when first they gazed on them.

2

The geographical background

One of the key facts of American geography is the mighty backbone of the dual continent—the range of mountains which extends from the Arctic to the Antarctic and claims some of the highest peaks on earth. In South America its name is the Andes; in North America, where it spreads itself more expansively, the major mountain chain is the Rockies. The mountains extend like a wall along the western margin of the continent, and in both North and South America vast plains extend eastwards from them.

In Middle America, however, the plains are largely absent. Their place is occupied by two seas, the Gulf of Mexico and the Caribbean, whose natural and perhaps former limits are marked by chains of island ramparts, the Antilles and the Bahamas. The western mountain wall itself is breached in several places in Middle America. There are gaps represented by the Isthmus of Tehuantepec in Mexico, by the depression partly occupied by Lake Nicaragua, and by the Isthmus of Panama. A none too dramatic rise in the level of the oceans would allow the Atlantic and the Pacific to mingle their waters over at least the last two of these frail barriers. Significantly, men have breached one, by constructing the Panama Canal, and have plans, shelved though perhaps only temporarily, for a second canal through the Isthmus of Nicaragua.

Middle America also has its lofty mountains. Costa Rica's highest mountain, Chirripo Grande, has an altitude of 12,589 feet, and its volcano Irazu is 11,326 feet high. Guatemala has Tajumulco at 13,616 feet and several volcanoes of over 12,000 feet. To the north-west, past the Isthmus of Tehuantepec,

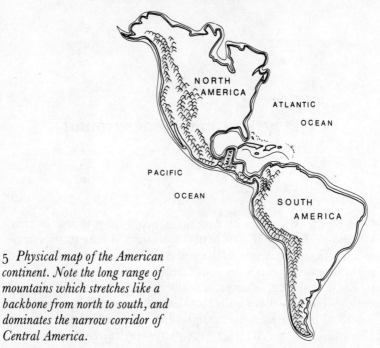

5 *Physical map of the American continent. Note the long range of mountains which stretches like a backbone from north to south, and dominates the narrow corridor of Central America.*

Mexico's mountains are even higher: Popocatepetl towers above Mexico City to the height of 17,887 feet, and Citlaltepetl, near Orizaba, to 18,701 feet.

Around the peaks are extensive tablelands, where most of the inhabitants of the Central American republics now live. Costa Rica has an average elevation of about 4,000 feet; the inland region of densely-populated El Salvador, away from the coastal strip, has an average altitude of over 2,000 feet; while Guatemala City and much of the land around it lies at an altitude of 4,800 feet. Although Central America lies within the tropics, the effects of latitude are therefore ameliorated by those of altitude, and the upland regions enjoy a climate of eternal summer.

Middle America has now been divided among eight countries. Of them, seven—Guatemala, Honduras, Belize (formerly British Honduras), El Salvador, Nicaragua, Costa Rica and Panama—lie wholly within the limits of the region generally known as Central America; while Mexico, the giant of the republics, has other territory extending far to the north. Each country, with the exception of Belize and El Salvador, has a

6 *A map of Central America, showing the extent of Maya territory and some of their near neighbours.*

coastline on both oceans. The heart of Mayan territory comprises much of Guatemala, Belize and the Yucatan peninsula of Mexico, but Mayan influence extends into Honduras and into other parts of Mexico, while the Indian tribes of the neighbouring Central American countries share many Mayan characteristics.

The Mayan heartland is a microcosm of the continents to the north and south. It has a high mountain zone to the south and west, along the Pacific coast (though here the coastline has been buckled around, so that it extends from west to east rather than from north to south). Between the mountains and the Pacific is a narrow, hot, coastal plain, but northwards and north-eastwards, on the Atlantic side, the plain is far more extensive. The peninsula of Yucatan, extending nearly 500 miles from the base of the mountains, comprises most of what is left of the submerged continental plains of Middle America. The Maya therefore occupied, and still largely occupy, a section of high plateau, studded with volcanoes and enjoying a temperate climate, a flat tropical plain, only a few feet above sea-level, and a gradation of country between.

In the mountains the climate is pleasant and the soil fertile.

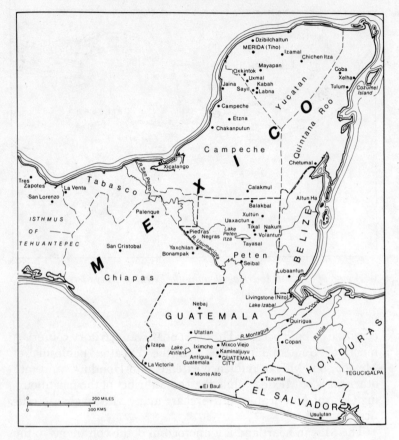

7 *The land of the Maya.*

The peasants grow maize for their own use and, today, coffee, of an excellent quality, for sale. In addition to the high volcanic peaks there are many pine-clad hills, reminiscent of Scotland, with good grazing land around the trees. The numerous deep valleys are well forested with deciduous trees closely related to those found in the forests of northern Europe and America. At least four species of oak are abundant, as are species of hawthorn, arbutus and buddleia. Rainfall is about the same as in western Europe or the eastern coastal region of North America, ranging downwards from a little over 40 inches per annum (1,170 millimetres).

Wild life in the highlands has been sadly diminished since

8 *This view of the partly excavated city of Palenque shows the dense forest beneath which so many Mayan sites have now been buried.*

classical Maya times. It seems likely that the forests then held many animals, such as jaguars and ocelots, which have since been virtually exterminated. Other smaller creatures, such as raccoons and opossums, which are better able to come to terms with the human occupation of their habitats, manage to survive, and several species of monkey still swing through the tall trees. Birds are numerous, but the highly-prized quetzal has never been common. This splendid bird, a member of the trogon family, inhabits the forest canopy of the mountains and is particularly notable for its tail streamers, sometimes as much as three feet long and shining in resplendent, metallic blue–green. Feathers were prized among the Maya, who were skilful at fashioning them into cloaks, headdresses, arm and leg bracelets and shield coverings;

the feathers of the quetzal bird, however, were reserved for persons of the highest rank. The quetzal lent its name to one of the chief Maya gods, Quetzalcoatl, and the present Guatemalan unit of currency is the quetzal. The bird is also depicted on Guatemala's flag.

The Maya were a Stone Age culture, and so placed a high value on stones that could be used for tools and other purposes. The volcanic highlands provided several deposits of great economic importance. For instance, the dark, glassy rock known as obsidian, formed by lava cooling quickly under relatively low pressure, was widely used to provide a cutting edge for tools and weapons. Jade, regarded almost with reverence by the peoples of Middle America and used for statues and ornaments, was found in certain mountain streams. Iron pyrites were cut into flat plates and fitted together to form multiple-lensed mirrors.

The central zone of Mayan territory comprises the whole vast expanse of undulating country from the foothills of the mountains to the low flat plains of Yucatan and the eastern sea. Even today from the air much of this countryside conveys the impression of unbroken, primeval forest. The population is sparse—the Guatemalan province of Peten, which lies in this region, extends over more than 14,000 square miles yet has a population of only about 65,000, and even that is more than five times what it was some 25 years ago.

The forest itself is an arboretum of tropical trees, of bewildering variety. Mahogany, Spanish cedar and sapodilla (from which chewing-gum is made) are probably the best known to the western world. And here wild life is much more plentiful than in the more densely settled highlands. Jaguars are still numerous. Herds of deer, peccaries and wild pigs roam beneath the trees, and the shy tapir browses in and around the swamps. High in the forest canopy, howler monkeys make the night echo with their roars, and sloths hang motionless from the branches. Though the quetzal is not found at these lower altitudes, the forests boast a wealth of colourful birds, including toucans, parrots, trogons and wild turkeys. Agouti, those giant cousins of the guinea-pig, come out at twilight to feed in forest clearings.

Although the forests are so extensive, there is also room in this vast territory for wide savannahs and numerous ranges of hills, the summits of which reach high above the forest cover. For instance, 20 per cent of Belize consists of land 1,000 feet or more

9 *Some of the hilly countryside in Chiapas, now part of Mexico.*

above sea-level, and much of Chiapas state, in Mexico, is very hilly.

The rainfall here, which is concentrated in the same seasons as in the highlands, is much heavier, reaching 120 inches a year in some places. As most of the land is almost uninhabited, the numerous streams and rivers are allowed to meander where they will and become silted up. In the rainy season, therefore, the countryside is to a large extent an amphibious realm, its swamps infested by mosquitoes, leeches and every kind of creature apparently designed to make life uncomfortable for man. Several of the rivers are quite large, notably the Usumacinta, which flows into the Gulf of Mexico, and the Motagua, which, striking farther south, mingles eventually with the waters of the Caribbean.

The third zone of Mayan territory consists of much of the peninsula of Yucatan. Here is a strange countryside of scrub and thorn, clothing a flat plateau not many feet above sea-level. The rainfall decreases as one descends from the southern hills, till in places it is less than 40 inches a year, which is little enough in a hot, tropical country with a high evaporation rate. There are few rivers, and the greater part of the peninsula is covered by a pervious layer of limestone, above which are only a few inches of soil. A remarkable feature of Yucatan is that in places the limestone shield has collapsed, pock-marking the landscape with holes which are really roofless caves. They give access to apparently unlimited supplies of water, created by the rain percolating through the limestone. The entire peninsula seems to be a limestone lid on a vast subterranean lake. Known as *cenotes*, these waterholes, some of them of considerable size, formed the main water supply of many of the Mayan cities. Their importance was all the greater because the rains were erratic, with frequent long periods of drought.

The lagoons which fringe the coasts of Yucatan, Tabasco and Belize played their part in the Maya economy. As well as supplying salt, which the Maya extracted by evaporating the water in shallow pans, the lagoons supported a large fishing industry. They also provided a habitat for the manatee, a marine grazing mammal which the Maya hunted. Turtles and iguanas were captured on the shores, and turtle eggs dug from the sand. Certain seashells were prized for ornament and also as a form of currency. There were pearl fisheries, though not on a very large scale. Dug-out canoes were used extensively, and the Maya also had open boats with sails capable of carrying up to 40 people.

The total area occupied by Maya covered about 120,000 square miles, roughly the same as the British Isles and rather smaller than California. One would have expected to find their greatest development in the well-favoured highland regions, but, oddly, that was not the case; it is in that zone that evidence of the more advanced achievements of the Maya is sparsest. Instead their civilization evolved and flowered in the central lowlands and, surprisingly, in the relatively inhospitable terrain of Yucatan.

10 *One of the Yucutan* cenotes, *into which the Maya used to throw gold, jewels and other treasures, including human beings, as sacrifices to the rain-god.*

3

The historical background

The first men to set foot on the American continent were doubtless unaware that they were doing so. They were almost certainly hunters following herds of caribou and mammoths eastwards from north-eastern Siberia over tundra that is now submerged beneath the Bering Sea. The likeliest period for the beginning of the trek was around 29,000 B.C., when, early in the Pleistocene Age, so much of the water in the northern seas was locked in a vast sheet of ice that the sea-level dropped by several hundred feet.

The migration into America was neither deliberate nor large-scale. Smaller family or tribal groups drifted, in the course of many generations, across the tundra in pursuit of game. The movement doubtless lasted for many thousands of years, until the 'land bridge' was eventually broken by the rising seas, and involved many peoples entirely unconnected with each other. They wandered on, with the passing of the centuries, until by about 9000 B.C. some had reached the Antarctic tip of South America.

The development of civilization on the American continent followed the same pattern as in the Old World. For millenia men gained their living by hunting and fishing, gradually perfecting new tools and weapons, such as grooved stone tips for hunting spears and woven nets for catching birds and fish. They also collected berries, seeds and roots in season. Among the earliest plants to be cultivated seem to have been squashes and beans, with maize, or corn, appearing soon afterwards. Maize, which grows plentifully in the wild in Central America, would be an obvious choice for women looking for seeds to grind. It was

11 *The staple food of the Maya was maize. These figures, found at Monte Alban near Oaxaca, are especially interesting since they indicate the use of corn at a very early period. The sculpture in the centre depicting ears of maize was probably a headdress.*

certainly under cultivation and making an important contribution to the diet of tribes living in central southern Mexico by 5000 B.C.

With cultivation Man ceases, after a time, to be nomadic. He puts a fence around his cultivated fields, builds a permanent house to live in, and combines with neighbours to form a settlement which is defensible against marauding animals and human enemies. Such villages grow into towns; and towns combine to form states. A surplus in the amount of food produced enables some of the citizens to specialize, in such varied spheres as weaving and religion, ironwork and oratory, art and soldiering. In Middle America the countryside seems to have been studded with farms and villages by about 2000 B.C. In the following millenium a number of tribes made parallel and more or less simultaneous advances towards civilization. Their origins and their relationship to each other remain obscure, though our knowledge of the period is steadily increasing.

EARLY INHABITANTS OF CENTRAL AMERICA

One of the most gifted and most enigmatic of these early peoples were the Olmecs, whose civilization sprang up, apparently suddenly, along the northern shores of the Isthmus of Tehuantepec around 1200 B.C. This is a little to the west of the indisputable Mayan area, but some authorities think that the Olmecs may have been a Mayan tribe. Through the mists which obscure the mysterious Olmecs we see emerging several characteristics of early civilizations that have their counterparts in the Old World and were later to develop considerably in America. Most important is the appearance of a social system dominated by priests and kings, perhaps often united in the same personages. Another interesting parallel with the Old World is the use made by the Olmecs of irrigation by the rivers which flow into the Gulf of Mexico. These, like the Nile, bring down silt after the rains, in floods which the Olmecs harnessed to their agriculture.

The Olmecs, like Stone Age peoples in other regions, undertook the transport of huge blocks of stone over considerable distances. Their favourite stone was basalt, quarried from the Tuxtla mountains, which run parallel to the coast. Archaeologists have found great basalt heads, often weighing as much as 20 tons. The Olmecs seem also to have invented the wheel, or to have acquired a knowledge of it from some outside source, and they mounted clay figures, apparently toys, to roll on wheels. Why they never developed this invention for practical purposes is still a mystery.

The Olmecs are thought to have been the inventors of the Long Count, the system of reckoning which enabled the Maya to become such proficient mathematicians and astronomers (see chapter 8). They are also credited with the invention of writing, again transmitted to the Maya. Clearly, the civilizations of the Olmecs and the Maya were intimately related, and many experts believe that they were simply different facets of the same phenomenon.

Before we enter the time zone of the full-fledged Mayan civilization it will be helpful to consider a few other early indigenous cultures of Middle America which influenced it. Near Oaxaca, capital of Oaxaca state in southern central Mexico, the hilltop of Monte Alban was occupied and levelled by the Zapotec people as early as about 600 B.C. The bas-relief sculpture known as 'The Dancers', on the huge masonry blocks in the foundations of a wall, belong to this early period. The great days of the Zapotecs came later, however, between 300 and 900 A.D., which coincides with the peak period of many of the Mayan cities.

Twenty-five miles north-east of Mexico City, the ruins of Teotihuacan were regarded by the Aztecs with some awe just

12 above *The Mexican city of Teotihuacan, which covered an area of eight square miles, was founded about the beginning of the Christian era. This photograph shows the Temple of the Sun, one of Teotihuacan's many great raised pyramids. Although not a Maya city, Teotihuacan had a strong influence on the development of Mayan civilization.*

13 right *An early carving from Monte Alban near Oaxaca, dating from about 200 B.C.*

before the Spanish conquest. Teotihuacan was a popular place of pilgrimage for the Aztec aristocracy who, however, had no knowledge of its history. To them it was 'the home of the gods', and they worshipped at the mouldering shrines. Teotihuacan, still an impressive site, was not, however, exceedingly old. It was probably founded about the beginning of the Christian era and was destroyed by invaders some 750 years later. Thus it was one of the civilizations that developed independently and more or less simultaneously with the Mayan.

Teotihuacan was not a Mayan city. For archaeologists, however, it provides a vital clue to the history of the area, for its influence is clearly traceable in the ruins of Kaminaljuyu, an early Mayan site on the outskirts of Guatemala City. Here, as at

Teotihuacan, are raised platforms crowned by temple pyramids; here are rich ornaments and painted pottery, much of it actually brought (no doubt on men's backs) from Teotihuacan itself, nearly 900 miles away.

Kaminaljuyu seems to have begun in a humble way in the fifth or fourth century B.C. and to have developed a brilliant culture by the first or second century A.D. Thereafter it declined a little, perhaps eclipsed by other Mayan cities farther north, and about A.D. 400 it fell under the control of Teotihuacan. The Teotihuacan invaders set about creating a miniature Teotihuacan at Kaminaljuyu, despite being handicapped by having only clay instead of stone to work with. Teotihuacan rulers definitely lived at Kaminaljuyu and were buried there, with great pomp and elaborate provisions for their future life. Their dominion seems to have lasted till Teotihuacan itself was destroyed, about A.D. 750.

Distant as is Kaminaljuyu from Teotihuacan it by no means marks the limits of Teotihuacan influence. Tikal, in the heart of the Peten and only 30 miles from the Belize border with Guatemala, also fell under the city's control. Tikal, like so many of the cities of the Mayan region, had its origins about 600 B.C. and eventually became the largest of all the Mayan cities. It has six temple pyramids, one of which is 210 feet high, and one scientist has estimated that its probable population at its zenith was 50,000. Stelae at Tikal dating from around A.D. 500 show Teotihuacan warriors and the Teotihuacan rain-god. But it has not yet been resolved whether this and similar discoveries are to be interpreted as evidence of trade or of conquest.

It is obvious, therefore, that the Mayan civilization did not evolve in a vacuum. All around the Maya lands were other related peoples, developing on parallel lines. Between them and the Maya there was a constant interchange of goods and ideas, both by trade and by war. Whether or not the Aztecs and the Incas had any knowledge of each other, the Aztecs and the Maya were certainly aware of one another's existence. The Aztecs, however, achieved power in Mexico when the Maya were already in decline.

A BRIEF SUMMARY OF MAYAN HISTORY

Students of Mayan history divide it into several periods as follows:

The *Formative Period* lasted from 1500 or 1000 B.C. to around

A.D. 150. During this time the Maya of the Guatemalan highlands and the Pacific coastal region seem to have developed most quickly, though towards the end of the period temples were being erected in Yucatan and the Peten.

The *Proto-Classic Period* occupied the years from A.D. 150–300, and laid the foundations of the brilliant Classic Period that was to follow. Some authorities dispense with the Proto-Classic period and consider it part of the Formative.

The *Classic Period*, extending from A.D. 300–925, saw the high flowering of the Mayan civilization, though from about A.D. 800 to 925 there was evidence of some decline.

The *Inter-regnum* lasted for some 50 years in the tenth century A.D., when Maya society sank to the cultural level which had prevailed approximately 900 years earlier.

The *Post-Classic Period* saw the revival of Mayan culture and the growth of new cities and city states, particularly in Yucatan. This period lasted until the Spanish conquest.

The independence of the Maya finally came to an end with the fall of the city of Tayasal, capital of the Itza people, in the Peten, in 1697.

It must be remembered that the early dating is almost entirely archaeological rather than documentary. It rests largely on a comparison of artefacts and styles. The earliest date recorded in inscriptions is the equivalent of 31 B.C., on a stelae at Chiapa de Corzo, in the Mexican state of Chiapas. This is outside the limits of strictly Mayan territory, though it uses the Long Count, a form of calendar afterwards associated with the Maya. The earliest inscriptions so far discovered in recognized Mayan lands are dated A.D. 292 and 320, dates on the threshold of the splendid Classic Period.

The Mayan sites of the Classic Period were not cities in the contemporary European sense but were primarily cult centres. The distribution of peasant dwellings in the immediate vicinity of the temple pyramids was only slightly more concentrated than in the more distant countryside. The construction of the cities' temples and palaces required stone, and it is natural that, given a fairly even distribution of population over the whole Mayan region, the cities should have proliferated where stone was most easily obtained and worked.

Two important Classic sites in the Peten were Tikal and Uaxactun. The ruins of Tikal, probably the most impressive of all

Mayan sites in Guatemala, cover more than 25 square miles. It has eight mighty pyramids, one of them 229 feet high, un-numbered stelae, palaces and altars (for no more than a quarter of the area has yet been excavated), and a grand plaza measuring 400 feet by 250 feet.

Uaxactun, only 35 miles away, is somewhat smaller but shares many of the same characteristics. Both are in low-lying, humid country, now densely afforested and very sparsely populated. The mosquito-infested jungles seem to us a poor place for the building of temples and civilized city-states. In the Mayan Classic Period, however, most of the land was probably cleared and cultivated, the clearing being, in any case, inevitable, if only to provide wood for lime-burning to make lime mortar. This material was used in the construction of nearly all Mayan buildings.

The earliest date mentioned on inscriptions at Uaxactun is A.D. 328; at Tikal, on the Leiden plaque which was found in the vicinity, A.D. 320, or, if one excludes that on the grounds that this may not have been its home locality, A.D. 416. These are the two oldest identified sites in the lowlands. Others with early dates include Balakbal and Uolantun, both of the early fifth century and both situated quite near Tikal. Later in the century the Mayan civilization spread outwards and by early in the sixth century had reached Chichen Itza, far in the north of Yucatan, and Copan, on the Guatemala–Honduras border. The expansion continued until nearly the end of the eighth century, by which time virtually the whole of the central and lowland Maya region was studded with temples and site centres (which for convenience are usually called cities, with the reservations already expressed).

The Classic Period which saw the expansion and florescence of the Mayan civilization is generally referred to as the Old Empire, but it was not strictly an empire. The Mayan political system was based on the independent city-state, in which respect it was similar to the organization of city-states in medieval Europe and classical Greece. Each state had as its head a hereditary ruler or chief. Military authority was in the hands of a war chief, who was elected for a three-year period. There was a hereditary priestly caste which was exceedingly influential. Certain authorities consider that, in some instances at least, the religious authority was combined, at its highest level, with the secular in the person of the hereditary ruler.

14 *Part of a stela bearing one of the earliest dates recorded on Mayan inscriptions, deciphered as 320 A.D. The stela was found in the city of Tikal, although it may not have originated there.*

Each state made its own alliances with its neighbours. The Mayan people, however, shared a common culture and religion and spoke related languages. A basis therefore existed for a closer political association, and this was achieved in the heyday of the Classic Period by a system of confederations, on much the same lines as the Hanseatic League or the league of Greek cities. Some of the largest cities, such as Tikal, gathered into their orbit a number of smaller centres, whose own chiefs served as an aristocratic caste to assist the chief ruler in the business of government.

As the civilization of the Classic Period gathered momentum, the principal Mayan cities sent out 'colonists' who deliberately founded other centres. It is probably more correct to think of these 'colonists', not as peasants setting out to form new agricultural settlements, but as priests and nobles establishing new centres of worship.

Paul Rivet, a great French authority on the Maya, asserts that between A.D. 534 and 633 the Maya founded ten new cities, five of them in the centre of their area and five on the fringes. One was the city of Tulum, on the distant eastern coast of Yucatan. In the next century 14 more new cities were added, among them Chakanputun, on the Gulf coast of Yucatan. Another period of expansion extended from A.D. 731–90, when three splendid new

25

centres were founded at Nakum, Seibal and Bonampak, all in the central region.

Soon afterwards decline set in. After about 850 few new sites were created and the older ones were gradually abandoned. As the tenth century wore on all the magnificent civilization that had been the Old Empire faded away.

Why this should have happened is still a mystery. There is no trace of the large-scale destruction and fires which would have marked an invasion or an earthquake. Geology suggests no dramatic change of climate. An epidemic is a possibility, but the two likeliest scourges, yellow fever and malaria, are thought only to have been introduced to the Americas at the time of the Spanish conquest. The explanation generally accepted at present is that the soil was exhausted by overcropping and wasteful agricultural techniques. Page 4 offers a personal experience of a tribe employing the slash-and-burn system. It is a technique which requires plenty of land. The very success of the Mayan civilization of the Old Empire could, by increasing the population and therefore the pressure on the land, have provided the seeds of its own demise.

The founding of new cities which characterized Mayan activity during the height of the Classic Period may have been motivated by a realization of the dangers of the situation. Viewed through the mists of more than a thousand years, the scene is one of swirling motion. New colonists are thrown out to the fringes of the settled territory, there to establish new centres; in the next century the activity moves back to the heartland and we see new cities being built there.

To give an instance the outline history of which seems fairly clear, the Itza people moved from the central Mayan area north-westwards into Yucatan early in the sixth century A.D. and there established the city of Chichen Itza, about 50 miles inland from the north coast of the peninsula. Nearly 200 years later (the recorded date is A.D. 692) they moved on 150 or 200 miles to found the city of Chakanputun, on the west coast. About A.D. 930 they started moving back again, accompanied by a warlike Indian tribe from central Mexico, who provided the leader, a man named Kukulkan. By 987 they were safely reinstated in Chichen Itza. Not content with occupying the old site, they founded several other cities, including Mayapan which became the last great Mayan 'capital', and, in 1007, Uxmal.

The civilization that grew up around these settlements, popularly known as the New Empire, represents the last brilliant flowering of the Maya genius. For 100 years or so Mayan arts and architecture flourished as in the great days of the Old Empire, or Classic Period. Then it was interrupted by civil war, the two chief protagonists being the citizens of Chichen Itza and of Mayapan. It seems that Chichen Itza was controlled by the Itza people, who were Mayan, while at Mayapan Indians from Mexico's central plateau were predominant. The latter called in mercenary auxiliaries from their homeland and finally defeated the Itza in 1194. Then, for some 250 years, relative peace prevailed. It was, however, a restless peace, for Mayapan seems to have ruled harshly. In 1441 the subject peoples revolted, killed their ruler and sacked the city of Mayapan.

Deterioration set in rapidly. Yucatan split into numerous little city-states, waging almost incessant war. Urban life declined, and with it most civilized arts. A destructive hurricane which hit the peninsula in 1464 hastened the process. Epidemics also seem to have played their part.

The Itza people decamped and trekked south to the neighbourhood of Tikal, where they occupied Tayasal, a site which they had abandoned in the ninth century. There, hidden by unhealthy jungles which were by then almost uninhabited, they retained their independence until 1697 (see page 116), when the Spanish commander, Martin de Ursaa, finally took Tayasal.

Such is a brief, perhaps over-brief, summary of Mayan history. Although the Mayan passion for the calendar has provided us with plenty of dates, the accompanying script has not yet been deciphered, and many of the events are subject to different interpretations by different experts. The situation is rendered more confused by the duplication of names; there are, for instance, two Kukulkans, separated by several centuries. The first of these heroes had, by a natural metamorphosis, become a god, and, to increase the confusion, Kukulkan in Mayan means exactly the same as Quetzalcoatl—'feathered serpent'.

THE SPANISH CONQUEST

The Spaniards first landed in Yucatan in 1511 but, being preoccupied with the much richer cities of Mexico, did not begin its conquest until 1527–8. The Mayan cities of northern Yucatan, then numbering 16 or 18 and in a state of chronic anarchy, were in no condition to offer an organized or united resistance. Nevertheless, they did not fall easily. Resorting to guerilla warfare, the Maya harassed the Spaniards for several decades.

After subduing and pacifying Mexico, Cortes despatched two of his lieutenants to deal with the kingdoms farther south. The able but ruthless Pedro de Alvarado was given the task of conquering Guatemala, which he did against desperate resistance. Here, as in Aztec Mexico, treachery and rivalry among the Indian tribes contributed to the Spanish victory. Guatemala, too, had its people who hated their neighbours worse than the Spaniards, whom they were prepared to help in order to settle old scores.

At the same time, another of Cortes's henchmen, Cristobal de Olid, was sent to subdue Honduras. De Olid, however, decided that this was a heaven-sent opportunity to set up a kingdom of his own. He reckoned without his commander. Starting from Tuzantepetl, near the northern coast of the Isthmus of Tehuantepec, Cortes, with a small army of Spaniards and Mexican auxiliaries, made an epic march across the unknown and harsh interior of Yucatan, to Nito, on the Caribbean coast. It was a desperate trek, through marshes, lagoons and jungles where, wrote Cortes, 'the overhanging foliage threw so deep a shade that the soldiers could not see where to set their feet'. Though his followers were ragged and fever-racked, the indomitable Cortes on reaching Honduras promptly put an end to the rebellion.

Then it was the turn of the Maya of Yucatan. Cortes's route had taken him across the broad base of the peninsula, through sparsely inhabited country. The remnants of Mayan tribes whom he found there told him they were descended from an ancient and mighty nation. Cortes also knew that in northern Yucatan there were cities and civilized men, though possibly not much gold. Francisco de Montejo was sent to deal with them.

Advancing from the west, Montejo met at first with little success. After his army had been broken down by a war of ambushes and attrition, he embarked on ships and sailed around to the other side of the peninsula, where he made a base at Chetumal. Driven from there, he took his flotilla down to Ulua, in Honduras, leaving the Maya victors in the first round. The campaign had begun in 1527 and it was now 1535.

Under Montejo's son a new campaign was launched in 1542. Thanks largely to internecine feuds among the Maya, it was

Ferdinandus Cortesius.

15 *Hernando Cortes (1485–1547), Spanish conquistador, who was responsible for the conquest of Mexico early in the sixteenth century.*

eventually successful. By 1546 the northern cities had been subdued, with horrific slaughter, and half a million Maya had been sold into slavery.

One Mayan tribe, the Itza, escaped by retreating to their ancestral home in the wastes of the Peten. There they maintained a small independent state until 1697. A Spanish missionary then negotiated the surrender of the Itza to a Spanish army, but at the last moment the truce was broken, by hotheads on both sides, and the last Mayan stronghold perished, as had so many other Indian cities, in a holocaust of fire and blood.

When all was over, the Maya settled down to a continuing sullen resentment against their conquerors. It is not, indeed, until the present century that many of the indigenous peoples of Yucatan have become at all reconciled to government by distant Mexico. Even now it is likely that resentment still smoulders in the secret Indian soul. That and apathy, bred by centuries of oppression and injustice, have militated against any revival of the old artistic genius of the Maya. There would seem to be no other reason why the present-day Maya should not have latent gifts as pronounced as those of their ancestors.

4

The people

Although, like all American Indians, the ancestors of the Maya apparently came to America via the land bridge which once existed where the Bering Sea now surges, anthropologists have difficulty in relating them to any surviving group in Mongolian Asia. Some authorities think that the Maya in particular have affinities with the Armenoid type, originating on the central tableland of Iran. If so, the uninitiated observer may be right in seeing a resemblance between the type represented in the Mayan frescoes and those of ancient Sumeria.

In one respect, the Mayan frescoes and bas-reliefs present a misleading picture. The men they depict appear to have long, narrow heads, the top of the skull being peculiarly elongated. In reality, the Maya were extremely brachycephalic—with broad heads in relation to their height. The distortion in the portraits, however, is actual, for it was the fashion to flatten and shape the heads of infants by binding them tightly to boards.

The frescoes, which tend to be realistic and often not at all flattering to individuals, show a wide range of physical types, from athletic, slim young men to paunchy old ones. Their skin colour is brown or copper, with black or dark brown eyes and hair. Contrary to a popular belief that there were no men with beards in America before the coming of Europeans, Mayan sculptures and paintings do occasionally depict men with beards and moustaches, though they are uncommon. The Maya have high, prominent cheekbones and usually straight or aquiline noses. Maya of Classic times, like most Mayan peasants today, were short, five feet being about the average height for men, with women four or five inches shorter.

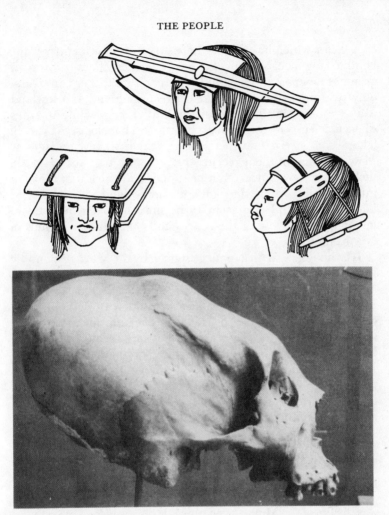

16 *The Maya used to flatten and shape the heads of infants by binding them tightly to boards. In the picture you can see some of the ways they did this.*

17 *A Mayan skull, showing the effects of the artificial flattening. This was thought to be fashionable.*

Throughout their history the Maya were in contact with other groups of Indians on all sides, particularly with the nations of Mexico. For long periods sections of the Maya were under the political domination of Mexican rulers. Under such circumstances intermarriages must have been frequent. The Maya are therefore as mixed a race as most European peoples.

A factor which has helped them preserve their identity is the bond of language. Volumes have been written about the Mayan group of languages. Some authorities hold that there are really only two major divisions, that between highland and lowland Maya, others that there are six main divisions, with numerous dialects. The distinguished British archaeologist, Eric S. Thompson, asserts that there are 15 major Maya languages or dialects, some of them recently extinct, and perhaps 23 in all, including minor dialects. But he supports the idea that they fall into two main groups, the highland and lowland Maya. Very far back there would also seem to be links between the Mayan languages and those of the Aztecs and other Indian groups of North America.

It is thought that the language spoken by the Maya responsible for the great architecture of Classic times was of the lowland group. Modern Yucatec is probably closest to it. The builders of 1,000 more years ago might still be able to communicate without much difficulty with the modern Maya of Yucatan, for most of the surviving Mayan languages are used by large groups of Indians. Indeed there may be as many as three million Maya-speaking Indians in their homeland today. The best estimates indicate that probably an equal number inhabited the Maya area in Classic times, though some authorities have suggested a population of as much as 13 million.

AGRICULTURE

The Mayan civilization was based on agriculture, with the principal crops being maize (corn), beans, sweet potatoes and squashes, with cacao and cotton as cash crops for trading. Maize was the life of the Maya. Even now it is the basic food at virtually every meal. Because of its supreme importance it was regarded with reverence by the Maya. It was not only a gift of the gods, it *was* a god. Indeed the Maya's obsession with the calendar probably arose from the necessity of accurately regulating the maize cycle.

The Maya felt an affinity, a sympathetic identification, with the maize plant. For it, as for them, life was hard. They had no draught beasts to assist them in cultivating the soil. Everything had to be done by manual labour, though in fact the actual stirring of the soil, as we understand cultivation, was almost non-existent. The preparation, sowing and harvesting of a field of

18 *Maize plants. Maize was the life-support of the Maya, and provided the basic food at virtually every meal.*

19 *This drawing from the Madrid Codex shows a god using a dibbing-stick to plant maize.*

maize was a communal effort by up to 20 men, chiefly because that was the most economical way of setting about it. First a patch of forest had to be selected and then cleared, a formidable task for men armed only with stone axes. This was done while the current crop was growing.

The climate of lowland Yucatan is divided into a season of heavy rains from late May to late August, with periods of light rain in January and February and in September and October. November–January and March–May are dry seasons. Tree ringing and felling were carried out either from August onwards, until it was interrupted by the November harvest, or in the dry season after harvest. Probably the earlier it started the better, for the brushwood and as much as possible of the trunks and larger branches had to be burned before planting could begin with the start of the rains in May.

The tool for planting was a simple dibbing-stick, its point hardened in fire. With it the Maya farmer made a hole in the soil four or five inches deep and dropped in several seeds, in the hope that at least one would grow and escape destruction by pests. With such a primitive technique, thorough clearing of the land was unnecessary—it was easy to plant the seeds round any awkward stumps that remained standing. Thereafter, the only tasks were to keep the land weeded as far as possible (a herculean undertaking) and to protect the crop against larger pests. Some of the bigger trunks and branches were built into a stockade to keep out marauding animals, but birds were a major nuisance, and, as in every tropical country, insects took a heavy toll.

The Maya seem to have appreciated to some extent the value of certain manures. They liked to plant their seed in the ashes of the burnt forest, and they knew that decaying bodies enriched the soil. 'The earth gives us food,' they said, as they buried their dead; 'we should feed it.'

The main harvest began in November but continued right through the dry season until March or April, as crops sown in succession during the previous rainy season ripened. The grain was stored in the village houses or in specially constructed granaries in the fields. Often, perhaps usually, a cleared field was cropped for a second year. Then it was allowed to relapse into jungle or forest, to replenish its fertility.

Victor W. Von Hagen, the historian and archaeological explorer, has made some significant estimates of the maize yields achieved by Mayan farmers. Today, he says, a Mayan peasant, cultivating about 12 acres, will harvest an average of 168 bushels of grain per year. On the assumption that the average Mayan family needs 6.55 pounds of maize per day (and this includes grain fed to domestic livestock), 64 bushels a year is consumed. That leaves a surplus of over 100 bushels, to be used for sale or barter. In producing this harvest the present-day Maya works for about 190 days, thus still leaving himself ample leisure. In Classic times the Maya peasant worked on the land for a considerably shorter period, partly because he had no draught animals to feed and partly because he cultivated a smaller area. As a result, although he produced probably less grain, he had much more leisure time. Von Hagen suggests that his work-days on the land totalled no more than 48 per year. The prolificacy of pyramids shows what he did with some of the rest of them.

The question of whether the peasant was a voluntary or

coerced partner in these ambitious building schemes is an open one. As already noted, the Maya peasant tended to identify himself with the maize which supported him. Every operation concerned with its planting and harvesting was controlled by religious ritual. Determining the correct days involved intricate calculations of lucky days and of days sacred to this god or that, with the rain-god taking preeminence. Even for the simple tasks that formed the basis of their lives, therefore, the peasants relied heavily on their priests. As we shall see when in a later chapter we look more closely at the religious beliefs and activities of the Maya, the whole vast, complex and brilliant fabric of mathematics, architecture, astronomy and other sciences achieved by the Mayan hierarchy rested on the basic need for an accurate calendar and, equally, for the ability to make accurate predictions. It may well be that a contributory reason for the abandonment of some of the religious sites was the failure of the priests concerned to make correct prognostications. A peasant people which spends all its leisure time building splendid temples to the gods in anticipation of future favours is entitled to expect results.

FOOD

Maize dominated the lives of the Maya women even more than those of the men. Its preparation and cooking occupied most of their time, for it is not an easy food to prepare. First it has to be shelled, and then partly cooked in order to facilitate the removal of the hard covering. Only after this can it be ground into flour. The flour itself was used in a variety of ways, most of which are still practised by the Maya and other American Indians today. One of the commonest forms in which it was served was as tortillas—flat unsweetened pancakes. They were cooked on platters of clay, placed over the three stones which formed the fireplace, and were served with a wide range of other dishes. As often happens today, a tortilla rolled into the shape of a pipe was used as a spoon, to scoop up other foods, and then was itself eaten at the end of the meal. A supply of tortillas was kept hot in a heated calabash, covered by a cloth.

Tortillas formed the basic food mainly at the evening meal, which was the chief one of the day. For a midday snack in the fields the men took dumplings of maize meal mixed to the consistency of a paste and wrapped in leaves to keep them moist.

They would mix these with water and flavour them with chillis or some other spice, or would eat them with meat if available. The morning meal, before work, would sometimes consist of tortillas and beans or, if supplies were running low, a kind of gruel, called *atole*, made by mixing maize meal in water and sweetening it with honey.

Although the Mayan diet was firmly based on maize it was fortified by a variety of other foods. Beans of several varieties were commonly cultivated and provided a valuable protein supplement. The well-known haricot or kidney bean is a native of tropical America. Sweet potatoes, which in addition to providing bulk starchy food are rich in Vitamin A, were extensively grown. Squashes, usually eaten boiled, also played an important part in the Mayan diet, and their hard shells were used for a variety of purposes, including storing food, carrying liquid, serving food at table and even making babies' rattles.

The Maya's favourite drink was chocolate, made from cocoa-beans which were roasted, ground and mixed with maize flour. The cacao shrub is indigenous to Central America. Cocoa-beans were prized as an article for trade and were widely used as currency. Most peasants regarded cocoa as a cash crop rather as one grown primarily for home consumption.

Mayan gardens grew avocado pears, pawpaws, guavas and soursops, all of which supply pleasant fruits. They had melons and mulberries, and also a number of crops grown for flavouring, chief of which was chilli (capsicum or pimento). In the jungle the men would collect vanilla beans from vanilla orchids, coriander for flavouring, and several leafy plants which could be cooked as spinach. Many edible varieties of fungi grow in the forests and were used by the Maya, though, as in other countries, the resemblance between poisonous and non-poisonous species is so close that great care had to be taken. Non-edible crops grown by the Maya included cotton and several agaves, or sisals, the fibres of which were used for weaving cloth. Fibres obtained from certain palm trees were woven into baskets.

The Maya had only one domestic animal (or mammal), the dog, one breed of which was hairless and was kept in confinement and fattened for eating. They had, however, several types of poultry, of which the chief was the turkey, raised in large numbers. Both turkeys and Muscovy ducks, which were widely domesticated, were valued almost as much for their feathers as for their flesh. The Maya also domesticated the yellow-crested curassow, a large turkey-like bird, and also several species of doves, which they fattened in cages.

Although today most edible mammals have been exterminated in the neighbourhood of settlements, in Classic times game seems to have been abundant. Mayan peasants combined hunting with farming and apparently often ate venison. Besides deer, agouti (large rodents), peccary (wild pigs), armadilloes, coatimundi and tapirs were hunted. Armadilloes were considered a special delicacy, as were manatees—large aquatic animals which feed on river vegetation. Iguanas and turtles were likewise prized.

In hunting, the Maya were assisted by dogs, of a different breed from those reared for eating. They were needed, for the Mayan peasant's armoury was, like his store of tools, decidedly meagre. Until the time of the New Empire he had no bows and arrows (these were introduced from Mexico in about the eleventh century A.D.) so he had to rely on his dogs and on clubs. For bringing down birds he had blow-pipes, used to shoot pellets of baked clay. The Maya were, however, adept at making traps and snares.

One possession of the Maya much envied by Europeans was a stingless bee. Many Mayan peasant households had bee-pots (usually hollowed tree-trunks) outside their houses. These produced large quantities of honey, and supplies were augmented by raids on the hives of wild bees. The honey was used for flavouring and sweetening dishes and drinks, and also for making a fermented drink similar to mead. The Maya mixed the honey with the bark of a tree and called it *balche*, a mixture more attractive to Mayan than to European palates.

Fish were taken by the Maya, both from rivers and freshwater lakes and from the sea. For catching fish from a stream the Maya would often build a dam and then place narcotic drugs, obtained from certain plants, in the water above the dam. When the stupefied fish floated to the surface they could be picked up by hand. In more extensive waters fishermen used both sweep and drag nets.

Present-day Maya eat snails, as no doubt did their ancestors. They also appreciate the larvae of a mud-wasp which makes a kind of cocoon of mud in which it lays its eggs. These mud nests are heated till the larvae wriggle out and are picked up.

20 top left *A terracotta figure from Jaina, showing a Mayan woman, with one child on her back and another watching her, preparing a tortilla.*

21 top right *A modern Mayan woman preparing a tortilla in much the same way.*

22 above *Detail from a mural in the Temple of the Warriors, Chichen Itza. The Maya were skilful fishermen, catching both freshwater and sea fish, and merchants also used large canoes to carry many of their goods.*

Three forest trees were of particular importance in the Mayan economy. Probably the most prized was the copal tree, the resin of which was used as incense by the Maya. Copal was an essential ingredient of the sacrifices and ceremonies that characterized Mayan religious life, and on virtually every occasion ordinary people were expected to bring gifts of it to the temple. Another important tree was the rubber tree, which yielded the raw material for the hard rubber balls widely used in ceremonial games. And the third was the sapodilla tree, which produces chicle, the raw material of chewing-gum and so of even greater significance in our civilization than in the Mayan. The Maya knew of it, though, and used it in much the same way as we do. They also used to chew the leaves of a plant, which they called *valapohov*, to quench their thirst.

It has been estimated that the Mayan peasant's average intake of food was about 2,500 calories a day, nearly 1,000 less than in the standard Western diet of today. The Maya would seem, however, not to have been under-nourished—judging from the number of plump bellies seen on the surviving frescoes. Their diet was reasonably well balanced, and the agricultural calendar allowed them ample leisure. In their tropical homeland, their lives must have compared very favourably with those of peasants in Europe at the time.

HOUSING

It seems somehow paradoxical that the Maya failed to lay out their cities in rectangular blocks, since this contrasts with their general preoccupation with squares. Their temple pyramids were built on a square base and stood alongside square or rectangular courtyards. Most of the houses were square or rectangular, though some of the rectangular ones had rounded ends. Mayan sculpture also tended to be square and chunky, and their hieroglyphic writing was arranged in straight rows of glyphs, each one rectangular with rounded corners.

In building houses the Maya naturally made use of local materials, and most of the lowland houses of ordinary people were of wood or woven withies, though often on a stone foundation. Early houses were frequently built on a low platform or dais, a feature magnified in the high platforms on which the temples were erected. In the highlands, where stone was plentiful, many of the houses had walls of rubbly stone. Lowland houses were almost invariably thatched with palm; but in the highlands grasses were used. Roofs were high-pitched, to shed the water of the heavy rains.

Mayan houses were simple, impermanent structures, not intended to last longer than a man's lifetime, if that. When a man

23 *A Mayan village scene, based on a mural in the Temple of the Warriors, Chichen Itza. Note the rectangular thatched huts; the simple dress of the peasants; the priest burning copal in a burner over the fire; and the men going off to work in the fields, carrying dibbing-sticks for planting maize.*

married he was expected to live near his father-in-law and to work for him for a number of years, so on his marriage a small hut was erected for him and his bride near his father-in-law's house. When the young man's term of service was over, he was helped by the community to build a larger hut to house his growing family. Members of the family who died were buried under the floor. Then when the father and mother died, the house was usually abandoned and served as a sacred shrine for the family.

There was little privacy in a Mayan house. Most buildings were divided into only two parts, by a wall or screen. One section was used as a kitchen, the other as sleeping quarters. Today Mayan peasants sleep in hammocks, but in Classic times they often used raised racks of woven withies on a timber frame. In the kitchen the stone hearth would be in the centre of the floor, the smoke escaping through the roof. There were wooden tables for holding storage pots, utensils and tools, and wooden stools for seats.

Classic Mayan houses lacked doors. At the most, a cloth or blanket was hung across the entrance, but usually the entrance was barred by a single string, hung with small bells, which gave warning when a visitor arrived. House-breaking and burglary were extremely rare, if not unknown, among the Maya. And they were probably so inured to communal life that privacy meant little to them.

The domestic life of the nobility, the priests and the merchants, is not well known. One of the earliest Spanish chroniclers, Bishop de Landa, described how 'before the Spaniards conquered the country, the natives lived together in towns in a very civilized fashion. They kept the land well cleared of weeds and planted very good trees. Their towns were arranged as follows: in the middle were the temples with their beautiful plazas; all around stood the houses of the lords and the priests, followed by the houses of the most important officials. Next were the houses of the very rich, and then those of the most respected merchants. At the edges of the town came the houses of the lower classes.'

The distinguished French archaeologist Paul Rivet, however, believes that 'the large centres, whose ruins have been explored by the archaeologists and which are called cities, were of an exclusively religious nature and were only inhabited by the most important priests and the civil chiefs.' Certainly excavations around the temples in the 'city' centres have failed to reveal the large houses in which rich and noble families might have been expected to live. On the other hand, the houses may well have been built of perishable material which has long since disappeared, while the clay platforms on which they stood have disintegrated and been washed away. Some stone buildings which were originally believed to have been noblemen's houses have proved on closer investigation to have been quite unsuited to permanent occupation.

Perhaps the answer is that each noble family would have a 'town house' for use when the head of the family came to the city for religious or state occasions, but that most of the time they lived on their country estates. Their food would be in substance similar to that of the peasants, though doubtless with some refinements and delicacies, and would be served by servants or slaves.

CLOTHES AND WEAVING

The flimsy, ephemeral structures that served, and serve, the Maya as houses are characteristic of the requirements of life in a tropical climate, where there is little need of protection from the cold. The same consideration applies to clothing. Mayan peasants wore very little. The men had a simple loincloth, or, rather, a band of material that went once around their waist and

24 above left *A terracotta figurine from Jaina showing a mother and child. Note their elongated skulls.*

25 above right *A bone pin, bone needle and stone spindle-whorl from Uaxactun. Weaving was one of the main occupations of Mayan women.*

then between their legs. Some at least possessed deerskin moccasins. And their wardrobe often included a kind of cloak, called a *pati*, which was thrown over their shoulders. The women had two garments—a length of decorated cloth with holes cut for head and arms, known as a *kub*; and a similar under-garment, which could be termed a slip or a petticoat, of lighter material. When not at work they often draped a stole over their shoulders. Both sexes also made use of a heavier square of cloth known as a *manta*, which served as an overwrap on cold days, and as a night-

26 *A detail from the Codex Troano-Cortesianus showing women spinning and weaving. This work was often done on a communal basis, in houses specially built for the purpose.*

time blanket. It was a *manta*, too, which was often hung as a curtain across the doorway.

Cotton and sisal were cultivated on a considerable scale, and weaving was one of the main occupations of Mayan women. Some authorities think, however, that cotton was reserved for use by the nobility and priests, and that common people made do with bark cloth. Women set about preparing fibres for weaving in their own homes, using spindles very like those developed in the Old World, but it seems that the weaving itself was sometimes carried on at looms in purpose-built weaving houses and was a communal operation.

While the dress of the peasants was simple, that of the nobility was much more colourful and elaborate. Mayan weavers made extensive use of dyes, dyeing the thread before starting to weave. Like their contemporaries in the Old World, they used both alum and urine to prepare dyes. Some colours were obtained from vegetable sources, such as red from brazilwood, green from avocado fruit, and blackish-purple from a kind of blackberry. Others had an animal origin, such as red from the cochineal insect, as in the Old World, and a deep purple, highly prized by the Maya, from the same mollusc that in the Mediterranean produced Tyrian purple. Yet others were obtained directly from minerals. Carbon yielded black; iron oxide, red; another oxide of iron produced yellow.

That civilizations in the Old and New Worlds should both have used dyes obtained from such apparently unlikely sources as a plant-sucking insect and a seashell has provoked speculation about a link between them. It is not a necessary inference, for

43

there have been other instances of simultaneous discoveries quite unconnected with one another. The origin of cotton poses another mystery. It was in use in both hemispheres in very early times—in India in about 2500 B.C., in Peru about 2000 B.C. Probably wild cotton, of various species, is indigenous to both regions.

Although their clothing was sparse, the Maya were fond of personal adornment. The ordinary people wore ornaments of bone, shell, wood and stone in their ears, noses and lips. For those of higher rank, the decorations were of metal or jade. Both sexes plaited their hair, in two or four plaits, which were sometimes coiled around their nape and sometimes hung down their back. On their forehead the hair was cut into a fringe. They also filed their teeth into points and sometimes covered them with plates of what were to them precious stones, such as obsidian, iron pyrites and, most valuable of all, jade.

Paint was used lavishly on their bodies, and was applied by means of pottery shards dipped in the paint pot. The colours had a significance. Warriors wore red and black; priests, blue; adolescents, black; slaves were striped black and white. As we note in a later chapter (page 90), colour had important religious and calendric associations. The blue worn by priests was associated with sacrifice, and so the victims themselves and the instruments with which they were immolated were also painted blue.

Tattooing was widely practised by the Maya. To be cross-eyed or squinting was considered fashionable, too, and to this end a ball of wax was often suspended from a child's forelock so that it dangled between his eyes. The absence of facial hair on Mayan men was probably due largely to deliberate depilation, begun by their mothers in childhood.

The dress and personal adornment of the aristocracy were an elaboration of those of the peasants. As in civilizations of the Old World, however, the higher the rank the more ornate the costume; the clothes and decorations worn by the top echelons precluded any possibility of the wearer ever doing any manual work. Mayan art is cluttered with a mass of detail, and the same principle was applied in decorating the persons of the highest officials in the state, notably the *halach uinic*—the king, or chief man. His face and body were tattooed. His nose was remodelled (or made up with clay) to give a high-bridged, aquiline

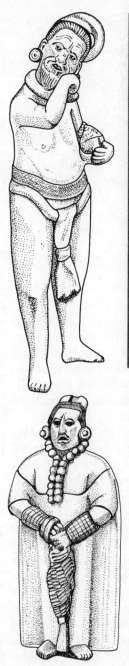

27 above left *A clay figure from Guaymil in Mexico (A.D. 900–1000). It depicts a peasant wearing a simple loincloth. However, even the poorest Maya liked to wear ornaments, and he has earrings and a necklace, and his hair is neatly plaited.*
28 above *A terracotta figurine from Jaina, probably a chief having a ritual bath before battle. Note the decorations on his face; tattooing was widely practised by the Maya.*
29 left *A Mayan noble of the Late Classic period. His head has been greatly elongated and his nose remodelled. He wears massive earrings, a heavy necklace and weighty bracelets and bangles. His breech-cloth bears an elaborate pattern but much of it is concealed beneath an ankle-length skirt. His coiffure is also carefully groomed.*

45

30 *Examples from Mayan art of some of the exuberant headdresses worn by the kings and nobles.*

appearance, and the left nostril pierced with a large hole in which a jewel (very often a topaz) was inserted. Similar huge perforations were made in the ear lobes, from which massive earrings were suspended. The early shaping of the head was pushed to extreme lengths, so that the top of the skull rose to a point. The front teeth, as well as being pointed, were inlaid with jade. Even the penis was trimmed to a 'fashionable' shape.

The belts and breech-cloths of Mayan nobles as depicted on murals are strikingly patterned. Sometimes they are concealed by ankle-length skirts. Over the shoulders the nobles wear cloaks, sometimes ankle-length, sometimes waist-length. Often jaguar skins are worn over the shoulders or suspended from the waist. The headdresses are outstandingly magnificent, even to the point of being grotesque. Those worn by the kings are sometimes larger than the man himself. They consisted of a frame on which were mounted exuberant effusions of feathers, chiefly the spectacular iridescent streamers of the quetzal, which were brought down to Yucatan from the mountains of Guatemala. Some of the nobles apparently sometimes wore cloth turbans. Others had headdresses with long, swirling, leaf-like appendages in imitation of the maize plant. Warriors, probably when preparing for or returning from battle, had their heads crowned by the masks of

31 *A terracotta figure of a warrior from Jaina. Note his massive earrings, his elongated skull, the bones used in his necklace, and the face on his shield which was supposed to frighten his enemies.*

jaguars and other animals, reptiles and fish, some apparently mythological.

Feathercraft was highly developed among many nations of American Indians. It was widely practised by both the Incas and the Aztecs, the latter keeping large aviaries of birds to supply the feathers; and the hunting tribes of North America, as is well known, made magnificent feather headdresses. The art reached its peak of florescence, however, with the Maya, perhaps because of the availability of such a wide range of brilliantly-plumaged birds. In addition to the quetzal, so highly valued that the unlicensed killing of one was punishable by death, there were toucans, trogons, motmots, long-tailed parrots, curassows, pheasants, jays, bitterns and many smaller species. Feathers were used to decorate cloaks and banners as well as for headdresses. Servants carried fans of feathers to brush away flies from their masters. Patterns of feathers were woven into skirts and the hanging ribbons of breech-cloths. Ceremonial shields were covered with feathers. Bands of feathers were used as knee ornaments and bracelets. Featherwork was the prerogative of women and, it is thought, particularly women of the upper classes. Each feather was patiently tied into the thread as it was being woven.

Noble ladies were distinguished from their humbler sisters by ornamentation similar to that which characterized the males. Like them, they had their heads excessively elongated, and they wore similar ear and nose jewels, as well as necklaces, bracelets and bangles. Their hair was arranged in elaborate coiffures, and a stole of a brilliant contrasting colour was often draped over a white *huipil*, or dress.

Our information about dress comes from literary sources and more particularly from mural paintings, of which many have fortunately survived. The hot, humid climate of Central America has made impossible the survival of actual fabrics, contrary to what happened in the arid coastal plain of Peru.

OTHER CRAFTS

The Maya were highly skilled in the art of modelling in clay and stucco, including the making of pottery, and their best work is equal to almost anything produced by the ancient cultures of the Mediterranean world. It is the more impressive because it was

48

32 left *A Mayan plaque depicting a noble in full regalia. The headdress and flowing cloak are made from the feathers of the quetzal bird.*

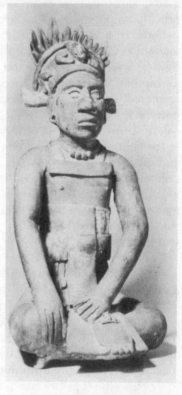

33 above *A woman with a tattooed face, from the Middle Classic period, A.D. 450–650. She is evidently an aristocratic lady, with her large ear-jewels, necklace and bracelets. Her hair-do is elaborate and she wears a fashionable stole over her dress (or huipil).*

34 above *One of the many fine terracotta figurines fashioned by Mayan potters. This one shows a man praying and comes from Jaina.*

fashioned without the aid of the potter's wheel. The Mayan potters worked with coils of wet clay, building up the vessel by winding round long strings of clay in ever-rising circles. When a sufficient number of coils had been added, they were smoothed and moulded into shape by human hand; then the potter finished off by going over the surface with a shard. Domestic pots and other utensils were made by pressing the clay into moulds, often decorated. Kilns were usually in the open air and were fired by wood or charcoal, or even grass.

The Mayan potters were women, who were thus entirely responsible for the lovely designs and superb craftsmanship of the very varied ceramic art. Enormous quantities of pottery were made, and surviving examples have been plentiful enough to provide ample material for a most detailed study of types and periods. In addition to articles for kitchen use, huge jars were made for storing water and others for use as braziers; incense-burners were in great demand for burning copal; earthenware drainpipes were widely used. Dead aristocrats were often cremated, and their ashes kept in funeral urns. Much of the pottery is lavishly and beautifully painted, the predominant colours being black, red, orange and grey.

In addition to the moulding of pots and pans, urns, beakers and pitchers, Mayan potters were extraordinarily skilful at fashioning figures. It is said, for instance, that every one of the 20,000 or so houses in the city of Mayapan had its household idol, made of baked clay. Workmanship ranges from crude primitives to remarkably realistic figures almost worthy of a classic Greek sculptor.

Ceramic experts have classified Mayan work as follows:

Mamom—primitive, utilitarian pottery, sparsely decorated, dating from 2000–500 B.C.

Chicanel—a more advanced type of ceramics, made between about 500 B.C. and A.D. 300. Colour and ornamentation were freely used, and well-executed figurines are numerous. The type appears to have emerged, fully-fledged, in the heart of Mayan Yucatan, without any transitional phase from the Mamom.

Tzakol—this type belongs to the Old Empire (A.D. 317–*c.* 650). The pottery is generously and colourfully decorated and tends to be cylindrical or round, often mounted on short legs.

Tepeu—dating from A.D. 650–1000, this illustrates the full flowering of Mayan art. The potters had complete mastery of their craft and allowed free play to their imagination. Articles are profusely decorated, with that same determination to fill every available space that characterizes Mayan sculpture.

Maya-Toltec—in this type the Mayan art of previous periods is merged with new ideas brought in by invaders from Mexico. It lasted until the coming of the Spaniards.

In this last period the only glazed pottery ever produced in ancient Central America, known as *plumbate*, was developed in the highlands of Guatemala, near the border with the Mexican state of Chiapas. It achieved a wide circulation over a short period, in the eleventh and twelfth centuries A.D., and for archaeologists serves the useful purpose of helping to date the strata in which it is found.

Associated with the Mayan skill in ceramics is their stucco work, which they used on a very large scale. Many of the pyramids were covered from base to apex with a shining coat of fine plaster. The Mayan mind being what it was, such a surface had to be covered, wherever possible, with paintings or carvings in bas-relief. Many pots and jars, too, were decorated with stucco work, which was applied after they had been fired. The Maya also used stucco for sculpturing. Among the treasures of the early city of Uaxactun are some towering stucco masks, eight feet tall. The greatest masterpieces in stucco, however, have been found in the city of Palenque, the palaces and temples of which have their walls decorated with hieroglyphics and with superb frescoes depicting Mayan life.

Stucco bas-reliefs and paintings alternate here, as elsewhere, with panels of relief work in stone, these too depicting scenes of daily life, conventional representations of gods, and hieroglyphics. Stone sculpture was achieved by tools no more advanced than basalt chisels and hammers. With these Mayan artists worked in stone as hard as marble, yet achieved a wonderfully sure mastery of line and texture. Despite the centuries of exposure to the tropical elements, many of the incised lines are still sharp and dramatic.

Among the most imposing monuments bequeathed to posterity by the Maya are the massive stone obelisks known as stelae. Consisting of a single stone and standing, in some instances, more than 30 feet high, they are carved in bold relief with figures, much as are the totem poles of Canadian Indians. They usually depict actual persons, such as kings and priests, and record in hieroglyphics the dates and presumably the events of their reigns. It was the custom of Mayan towns to erect such stelae at regular intervals—first every 20 years and then, in later times, every 5 years. The art of erecting and sculpting stelae was at its height during the peak years of the Old Empire (633–731) and seems to have come to an end with the decline of the Empire towards the close of the ninth century A.D.

Later the technique was revived, though briefly and without the old mastery. A new form of sculpture also appeared at the city of Chichen Itza, where there are many figures carved in the round and used as supports. Some are human figures, which have been appropriately named Atlantids and which support altars on their raised hands, like Atlas. Others, known as standard-bearers, crouch to hold the poles of standards between their hands and their feet. Stone jaguars form the base of thrones. And, most interesting of all, stone figures of men, half lying and half resting on their elbows, once supported something, apparently a large bowl, on their stomachs. These are called Chac Mools, and there are a dozen or more in Chichen Itza alone.

Carving in wood, like modelling in clay, probably preceded the art of carving in stone. Thus it is not inappropriate to compare the Mayan stelae with Canadian totem-poles—in all probability the earliest stelae were made of wood. Wood was used not only for domestic utensils and tools, but also for temple idols, a particular wood, Spanish cedar, being reserved for making images of the gods. Some panels of wood carved with scenes of Mayan life and with hieroglyphics have survived in the interior of temples and palaces and demonstrate a remarkable mastery of woodwork. There are particularly striking examples, in sapodilla wood, on ceilings in Tikal. Other wooden objects have been recovered from the depths of sacred *cenotes*. Wood was also used to make the carved masks for priests and actors, military helmets, and the covers for books.

Almost all sculpture, whether in wood, stone or clay, was painted. The Maya loved colour. Much of our knowledge of Mayan custom and costume derives from the magnificent paintings that adorn the interior walls of temples, notably one at Bonampak, in the south-eastern corner of Chiapas. Bonampak was one of the cities founded in the great period of expansion of the Old Empire, from A.D. 731–90. The murals adorn three rooms and are painted in vivid colours on a layer of lime plaster.

They date from about A.D. 800 and evidently record a successful campaign undertaken by the town against a neighbour. The paintings are reminiscent of the best Egyptian tomb paintings but are livelier and more dramatic.

The murals and frescoes were probably executed by a class of lay artists attached to the priesthood. Their work was not intended to be seen by the general public but was for the eyes of the hierarchy alone, or perhaps even just for the gods. In one of his reconstructions of scenes of Mayan life, Eric S. Thompson suggests that a novice who made a careless mistake in fashioning

35 *A detail from one of the murals of Bonampak, showing men fighting in a tribal war. The colours are extremely vivid, and the artist used the same technique in representing figures as is found in many of the Egyptian tomb paintings.*

a glyph or a religious theme might well find himself on the sacrificial altar of the god.

The Mayan civilization was a Stone Age one. The Maya had not discovered how to make bronze, though they did sometimes use copper which, however, had to be imported. So did gold, the chief source of which seems to have been Panama. Consequently metalworking was not a craft of great importance among them. They did fashion copper into ornaments and into the little bells which they strung across house doorways or used as bangles. Most gold objects, recovered from the sacred *cenotes* into which they had been thrown as offerings to the gods, were evidently imported ready-made, although in the time of the New Empire there seems to have been a small industry in making ornamented discs of thin beaten gold. Gold and copper were used as offerings to the gods, but they do not seem to have been prized for the intrinsic value of the metal. It is even said that both metals were used for such a mundane purpose as fish-hooks! Just before the arrival of the Spaniards, however, the Maya seem to have become conscious of the usefulness of metals as a currency in trading. The conquistadores found a few caches of gold in the coastal towns of Yucatan.

For the Maya, however, jade was of considerably greater value than gold. Its source is unknown, but it is thought to have been obtained from the beds of mountain streams. It was rare enough for the Maya to prize it almost as much as the Spaniards did gold. Jade, a silicate of magnesium and calcium, is a very hard stone, and working it calls for a high degree of skill and patience. Having no metal tools, the Maya craftsmen cut the jade by rubbing quartz sand into minute depressions on its surface. The original line was made by working a cord of twisted vegetable fibre endlessly to and fro. Mayan lapidaries also used obsidian tools. Drills made of bone or hardened wood were employed to make holes, which were enlarged by twisting in them drills of increasing size, with an admixture of quartz grit and water to make the tools more effective. With such primitive aids the Mayan craftsmen produced masterpieces both in the round and in bas-relief. A magnificent jade head of the sun-god, Kinich Ahau, discovered in a tomb at Altun Ha in Belize, stands 6 inches high and weighs 9¾ pounds. Another from San Jeronimo, in Guatemala, stands 10½ inches high and weighs 12½ pounds. Bas-relief figures on a jade plaque dating from about A.D. 750, and

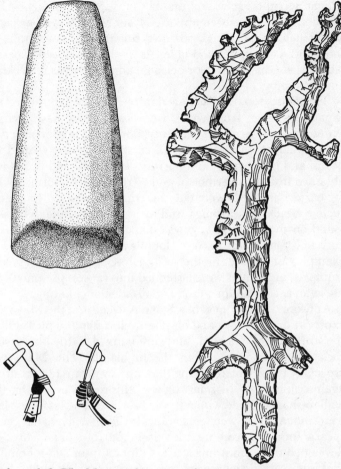

36 above left *The Mayan culture was a Stone Age one, and Mayan craftsmen were expert at fashioning tools from stone, especially the hard stone known as obsidian. Here is a stone axe from Uaxactun, together with drawings, taken from the Madrid Codex (left) and the Dresden Codex (right), showing how it was fitted into a handle and wielded.*
37 above *An 'eccentric' flint which has been carved to represent two human profiles. The Maya were extremely skilful at this strange art.*

found at Nebaj in Guatemala, are alive with flowing movement.

Jade was also used, in conjunction with iron pyrites and turquoise, to make mosaics. This may well have been an art that originated elsewhere, however, for some of the mosaics found on

55

Mayan territory, such as a number of discs from Chichen Itza, are thought to have been imported from Mexico. A stone jaguar at Chichen Itza, originally painted bright red, has its numerous spots and its eyes of inlaid jade. As might have been expected, jade was also in demand for personal adornment, as in necklaces and pendants.

Turquoise, too, was fashioned into jewellery and ranked next to jade in value. Iron pyrites were used, as we have seen, for capping teeth—as an aid to beauty, not for the sake of preserving the teeth. Iron pyrites and rock crystal were also shaped into beads, and iron pyrites into mirrors. Both coral and pearls were obtained from the Caribbean and were used for adornment and for barter. Seashells were cut and trimmed to form ornaments, such as beads and earplugs, and the spiny pink Spondylus shell, found on the Pacific coast, was shaped into beads and used as currency. Shells were also used for inlay work, and there are a few examples of carved mother-of-pearl. Conch shells served as trumpets, and others were fashioned into rattles, presumably for use as an accompaniment to religious song or chanting.

Appropriately for men of a Stone Age culture, the Maya were expert at dressing flint and obsidian. Flint is found plentifully in the lowlands of Yucatan, and obsidian—a hard, black, shiny rock of volcanic origin—in the highlands. The Maya were especially proficient at flaking the stone by means of pressure (as against chipping it by smart blows); this results in a wafer-thin, scallop-shaped blade with a rippled surface. The leaf-like blades were mounted in wooden handles to form knives, daggers or spearpoints, and were used for tipping arrows. The Maya also developed the extraordinary art of flint sculpture, fashioning the flint into fantastic foliated shapes, bearing fanciful resemblances to men with exotic headdresses, scorpions, dogs and the plumed serpent that is a favourite theme of Mayan art.

38 *A flint arrow-head and knife from Uaxactun. The leaf-like blades were mounted in wooden handles.*

5

The cycle of life in a Mayan village

The day began before earliest light, when the women arose, stirred the fire and began making preparations for breakfast. Fire was obtained by twirling a stick with a hardened point in a cavity in soft wood, which acted as tinder, but this was not a daily exercise since the ashes under the three-stone hearth normally kept hot all night.

Preparation for breakfast was a somewhat lengthy affair; although beans were left in the pot overnight, a new batch of maize had to be ground each morning. The maize grains were kept soaking in lime-impregnated water all night, to soften the hulls, which had to be removed before grinding could begin. The grinding was done by rolling the soft grains on a flat stone with a stone rolling-pin. The end product was a paste or dough rather than flour, but of just the right consistency for making tortillas. These were baked on an earthenware griddle and then dropped, while hot, into a calabash, covered with a cloth to keep them warm.

39 *A detail from the Madrid Codex showing a merchant god making fire. The Maya obtained fire by twirling a stick with a hardened point in a cavity of soft wood.*

57

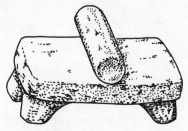

41 *A grinding stand and stone rolling-pin used for preparing maize. Found in a burial at Balancanche, Yucatan.*

40 above left *Grinding maize. The grains were first softened by soaking and then ground on a flat stone with a stone rolling-pin. This drawing is based on a pottery figurine found at Lubaantun. The woman carries a child on her back.*

While this was going on, the man of the house was about his morning devotions. Taking some embers from the fire for his incense-burner (an earthenware container), he squatted outside the hut, facing east. As he dropped little lumps of copal into the burner and watched the fragrant smoke curling up he prayed for good hunting, or favourable planting weather, or rain, according to the needs of the coming day.

When the tortillas were ready, the man came back into the hut and, sitting on a log stool, dipped into the calabash. Each tortilla was twisted into the form of a spoon or scoop which enabled him to dip into the pot for a mouthful of beans. Eating the 'spoon' with its contents, he thus obtained a nicely balanced diet of protein and carbohydrates!

The custom of early rising was dictated by the tropical climate, which required that work should be done during the cooler hours of morning and, perhaps, evening. In the heat of the day, the Maya preferred to rest. Also, of course, if it was a day for hunting, the best chance of success lay in the hours immediately before and after dawn. When hunting, the man would take his lunch, in the form of maize dumplings wrapped in a leaf. If he was working in the fields, his wife would usually bring his lunch out to him.

The evening meal was taken at about five o'clock. Before he sat down to it the man enjoyed his daily bath, normally a hot one, taken in a wooden tub, for which his wife had been heating water all day in earthenware pans over the fire. In the bigger cities, such as Tikal, he could alternatively visit the communal steam baths and sit there talking with his friends.

The five o'clock meal was the most elaborate and substantial of the day. Tortillas again formed the basis of it, but instead of beans the women would serve whatever meat or fish was available, usually in the form of a stew, together with herbs and vegetables. If flesh were scarce, eggs might be used as a substitute. For dessert the peasants had a wide variety of fruits in season. Their main beverage was chocolate, made from cocoa-beans and maize flour, which the early Spanish chroniclers described as a very pleasant, foaming drink. In the absence of cocoa-beans—and they tended to be expensive in Yucatan, having to be brought in from the hills—the family would drink a mixture of water and maize meal, perhaps sweetened with honey. To drink pure water was unusual.

The evening was spent either in conversation with friends and neighbours or in handicrafts. The man would make or repair tools while his wife spun or wove. Alternatively they might engage in making artefacts to be sold at the local market. At some time during the evening the wife would put the next day's ration of maize to soak in jars of lime-water. The evening meal—a light one similar to breakfast—would be eaten at eight or nine o'clock, after which the family went to bed.

The cycle of Mayan agriculture consisted mainly of growing maize. From the cleared fields each family was allocated a plot of 400 square feet, but clearing the scrub and cultivating the land was a communal task in which all shared. Work in the fields was concentrated into certain busy periods, as in most tropical agriculture. The intense activity of brush-clearing, planting, weeding and harvesting would be followed by long intervals of comparative leisure. As mentioned on page 34, the essential work of a Mayan farmer occupied him for only two months out of twelve. He had ample time left for building pyramids, hunting, craftwork, making war and enjoying seasonal festivals.

MARKETS AND TRADE

Mayan peasants would also, from time to time, attend the local market. For information about old-time Mayan markets we have to rely on the accounts given by the early Spanish chroniclers, in whose time only the towns of northern Yucatan were still flourishing. One of the biggest of all markets was at Chichen Itza, the essential features of which are described by von Hagen as follows:

> Within the court of the thousand columns in the Temple of the Warriors is a large area which Landa called the *mercado*. Open on four sides, it had a thatched roof supported by tall stone Doric-like columns, which still stand. There are also remains of a stone dais, on which the official sat to administrate sales and trading. In the open courtyard, squatting under white cotton awnings, men and women bartered the goods that they created in the surplus time allowed them by the cultivation of maize. In appearance it probably did not differ from the Aztec market so often described. Each product had its place. There was a section where fish, deer meat and birds were sold. Cloth and cotton dealers had their precise area as did those who traded in plumes, arms and the other items of commerce.

The Mayan markets did not, in fact, differ greatly from those in many other parts of the contemporary world. Nor would it be difficult to find their counterpart in much of tropical America, Africa and Asia today.

Eric S. Thompson suggests that a market held every five days might be usual in an ancient Mayan city. 'A Mayan city,' he writes, 'was not a city at all in our sense of the word, because it was a ceremonial, not an urban, centre, to which people repaired for religious ceremonies, civic functions and markets.' He visualizes the houses around the city centres as being town houses for persons normally resident outside the town, or, perhaps even more likely, as storehouses for the things needed for worship or ceremonial occasions. At the conclusion of such a celebration, he suggests, would come 'a general exodus from temple and palace back to everyday life. The city would lie deserted except for those who swept the courts and buildings or stored the masks and vestments, and for priests on tour of duty. Then at the next market day the city would come alive again. Buyers and sellers, their business done, would come to gaze and make their offerings at humbler shrines; persons of rank, borne in litters, would worship secludedly at the great shrines or gather for a council of state; a game of ball would be going on with many onlookers crowding to see the play; and perhaps dancers decked in fantastic masks would weave their patterns on some sunlit court to the sound of drum and flute.'

Thompson points out that this reconstruction is based not only on archaeological and documentary evidence but on what goes on today in some Mayan communities in Guatemala. 'In places the present-day Maya live in scattered settlements covering a wide area, where they have their cornfields and where they carry on their normal activities, but they also have their town houses, to which they repair for important religious functions . . . and for such civic events as the installation of new communal officers and markets. The modern town, in fact, functions very much as we have supposed the old Maya cities did, save that family houses now invade the centre. Between ceremonies the town is largely vacant.'

Certainly our typical peasant would have been a spectator rather than a participant in the major ceremonies. To the market he would have taken his surplus maize, beans and vegetables. One of the most important items of trade was salt. This was a speciality of the coastal regions of Yucatan, where it was obtained by evaporation from the numerous lagoons. It was exported far and wide and paid for many of the imports which the cities of Yucatan needed, particularly cacao. Much trade was transacted by barter, but cocoa-beans formed a convenient and frequent form of currency. They were in such demand that counterfeiting cocoa-beans was one of the commonest crimes judged in Mayan courts. Unscrupulous merchants stripped off the husks of cocoa-beans, filled them with sand and mixed them up with genuine beans. Wide-awake customers formed the habit of squeezing each bean, to make sure.

The Maya were great traders. They travelled by sea, by river (navigating their largest river, the Usumacinta, for 240 miles from its mouth), and by a well-constructed road system (see page 132). By land, everything had to be carried on human backs, for the Maya had no beasts of burden and no wheeled vehicles. The cities of Yucatan needed to import obsidian, jade and other semi-precious stones from the highlands, also quetzal feathers, copal and, of course, cocoa-beans. For sale they had salt, cotton and cotton goods, honey, dried fish, seashells and the skins of animals. Traders, who were highly regarded and afforded protection on their journeys, besides being generally exempt from taxation, went far beyond the bounds of Maya territory, penetrating at

42 above left *A detail from a mural in the Temple of the Warriors, Chichen Itza. The Maya had no beasts of burden, and all their merchandise had to be carried, usually on the backs of slaves.*

43 above *A sculpture from Piedras Negras showing a prisoner of war. Judging from his headdress and decorations he is of high caste and so would probably be sacrificed to the gods rather than directed into slavery.*

44 left *The Maya used slaves for all the hard and menial tasks. This relief from the Temple of the Sun at Palenque shows a priest offering sacrifice standing on the back of a slave.*

least to Mexico in the north-west and to Panama in the south-east.

One article of commerce which has no equivalent in modern Central America is slaves. The incidence of slavery among the Maya is difficult to determine, but their art depicts numerous persons who are evidently slaves, and the early chroniclers refer to the practice as widespread. Slaves, it would seem, were sometimes hereditary but were also recruited from three main sources. A family experiencing hard times could sell off surplus children into slavery, and orphans were often co-opted to join the slave force of a household. War prisoners of humble status were directed into slavery (those of higher rank being reserved for sacrifice to the gods); and slavery was also a legal punishment for serious crimes.

Slaves were required to do much of the hard manual work of well-to-do households. They carried merchandise on their backs, paddled canoes, fanned flies away from their exalted masters, collected the noxious materials used for dyeing, and ground maize meal. The market price of an adult, able-bodied slave at the time of the conquistadores was, incidentally, 100 cocoa-beans. Slaves were, it seems, not badly treated, but when an important person died his slaves were often knocked on the head and buried with him. They were also frequently pressed into service as a sacrifice to this god or that, unless the need for divine favours was desperate enough to call for the offering of a free man.

RELIGIOUS CEREMONIES

Just as in medieval Europe all holidays were religious festivals or saints' days, so with the Maya all festivals, like almost every other aspect of life, had religious associations. Commercial markets and fairs, fiestas and revels, and religious ceremonies were all closely interconnected. Dancing, as with most primitive peoples, was a religious exercise. The Mayan ball games, too, had a religious significance. Each of the 18 Mayan months had its own round of ceremonies and feasts. Although preparation for many of them involved a fast, most culminated in a gluttonous feast at which the male participants usually got drunk. Some were unequivocal orgies. There seems, however, to have been little scope for spontaneous expression of feelings by Mayan villagers in the form of dance, drama or music. These were all the preserve of professionals, working under the auspices of the priesthood,

45 *A scene from a modern Mayan market at San Cristobal de las Casas, in Chiapas, Mexico.*

and the ordinary people had to be content with the role of spectator.

Even ball games, to which the Maya, like other Middle American peoples, were passionately addicted, had close religious associations, though it is likely that they were also engaged in for recreation. A feature of nearly all Mayan cities is the ball court, a long rectangular enclosure surrounded by tiers of seats for spectators. In the middle, at surprising heights sometimes of 20 or 30 feet, a stone ring was set, and the object of the game was to direct the ball through this ring. The ball, made of rubber, was some six inches in diameter and light enough to bounce well. The players were only allowed to hit it with their buttocks, fists and elbows. They wore protective gloves and belts. Scoring a goal by getting the ball through the nearly inaccessible ring must have been so rare an achievement that much of the attention must have been focused on the secondary purpose of keeping the ball in motion for as long as possible. Action was so rapid and so prolonged that even the most athletic players sometimes fell utterly exhausted.

Direct information about the game as played by the Maya—they called it *pok-a-tok*—is meagre, but it may be assumed that it was much the same as the Aztec version, which is

46 *The stone ring from the ball court at Chichen Itza. The ball players, using only their fists, elbows and buttocks, tried to direct a rubber ball through the ring high on the wall. The Maya took their national game very seriously; indeed, the losers in an important match were sometimes sacrificed.*

47 *For the Mayan ball game, called* pok-a-tok, *the players wore protective gloves, hip-padding and belts. The games had a religious significance and expert players became very popular. The drawing is from a clay figurine found at Jaina and dating from the eighth century* A.D.

more fully recorded. Among the Aztecs any player who achieved the rare feet of bouncing the ball through the ring was entitled to claim the jewellery and clothing of all the spectators—provided he could catch them! The spectators gambled on the outcome of the game, placing immense bets including 'gold, turquoise, slaves, rich mantles, even cornfields and houses'. Among the Maya success or failure seems sometimes to have had even more sinister implications. Thompson records that on a relief at Izapa, on the Pacific coast, 'the decapitated man has his right hand gloved, indicating that he was a defeated ball-game player. The victor, severed head in hand, stands over him.' A similar scene is depicted in relief on a ball-court wall at Chichen Itza.

No doubt youngsters in the villages played their own version of the ball game without the benefit of a special court. They also played with bows and arrows and with barbed spears, and had a game something like chequers, played with beans on a marked board.

SOCIAL ORGANIZATION

Mayan villages generally seem to have been organized on the lines of a clan system. Although each family had an allotment of land, a group of 15 or 20 neighbours would combine to tackle the main agricultural tasks, and most of the inhabitants of a village were probably related.

The Maya in general took pride in their genealogy. They measured it both patrilineally and matrilineally. Each person had two names, one derived from his father's family and one from his mother's. Property and membership of the 'clan' which engaged in mutual help descended through the male line. The implications of relationship in the female line were mostly concerned with marriage taboos. A man could not marry a woman bearing the same matrilineal name as himself, even if she were not closely related, whereas he could marry a closely-related woman, even a first cousin, provided she did not bear his name.

It would have been most unlikely for such a compact, well-organized society to flourish without a social hierarchy battening upon it, and the Maya certainly had their hierarchy in good measure, as well as an associated bureaucracy. Each Mayan village or settlement came under the control of a lord, to whom taxes of various kinds were payable. These taxes were twofold: on produce, and in personal service. A proportion of all the crops harvested had to be paid over to the state. This was stored in warehouses and later distributed to the non-productive members of society, including the priesthood. As in feudal Europe, the peasants also had to cultivate the fields of their lords, and, in this instance, of the priests too.

Village communities were required to maintain the highways near their homes, and they had to build and keep in repair the houses of the priests and nobles. The splendid and profuse architecture of the Mayan cities, the temples, tombs, ball courts, reservoirs and other impressive structures, were also built by peasant labour. Moreover, when a Mayan lord travelled outside his own domain, he took with him a large retinue of retainers, partly for prestige reasons and partly to carry the baggage.

The exaction of all these dues was the function of an immensely powerful official, the *batab*. To the Mayan peasant the *batab* must have represented supreme Authority. He travelled in regal state, with an army of retainers and personal attendants. When he alighted from his litter cloaks were spread on the ground for him to tread on. A Spanish captain who was granted an interview with a *batab* found he had to speak to the exalted person through a screen of cotton cloth. In addition to collecting taxes, the *batab* acted as a judge in all but the most important disputes that arose within his administrative area. Occasionally he would conduct sacrifices. And, in time of war, it was the *batab* who led his levy into battle.

The *batab* had beneath him a whole civil service of deputies. At village level, his dealings would be with the headman of the clan rather than with individual villagers. It must not be thought, however, that these tributes were exacted from an unwilling peasantry. Obsessed as they were by a religion intimately connected with the calendar, the Maya peasants relied on their priests to guide them in all their activities, particularly those associated with the growing and harvesting of crops. One of the *batab*'s main tasks was to relay the priests' instructions concerning favourable and unfavourable dates. These instructions were assumed to come directly from the gods, who were thus intimately involved in the production of the essentials of life. If, then, the gods demanded temples, the peasants willingly complied. One good turn deserved another. In any case, temple-building itself was controlled by the calendar. The time for the construction of a new temple came round as regularly as the time for sowing and the time of harvest and so was taken for granted. People tend to accept without question anything that has become a custom.

Whether the peasants regarded the other dues demanded from them as excessive we do not know. They may not in fact have been any heavier, in their entirety, than the taxes paid by a citizen in a modern state. As we have seen (page 34), the cultivation of the maize crop need not have occupied more than 48–50 days in the year, leaving ample time for other activities. Doubtless the ruling classes argued that to keep the peasants busy was to keep them out of mischief. As for the tribute in kind, von Hagen quotes the instance of one small village of 20 households which annually paid its lord some 1,200 pounds of maize and about 20 turkeys. If this burden were equally distributed, each household would be called upon to contribute 60 pounds of maize and a turkey. That would seem to be a reasonable imposition, which it could manage without hardship in a normal year.

Peasant grievances, if they existed, were more likely to be based on comparisons. Hardships can be accepted when equally borne; ill-feelings are only engendered when privileged persons can be seen to be escaping scot-free. In Mayan society there were large numbers of people who were exempt from taxation. They included all the nobility, all the priesthood and all the civil servants and army officers. In fact, only the peasant paid. Even the merchants, who were a class apart, paid no dues, on the grounds that the risks they took entitled them to the large profits they often made.

In spite of this underlying cause of discontent, Mayan society generally seems to have functioned smoothly. Even war did not unduly disrupt it, war being accepted as a natural phenomenon. The only occasion when the peasants were upset was when their religion failed them—in other words, when the priests made an error in calendric predictions. A loss of faith could be caused by a failure of the rains. Having followed precisely the instructions of the priests, via the *batab*, regarding the preparation of their fields and the sowing of the maize, the peasants would feel they had the right to expect cooperation from the gods in sending rain at the proper season. Probably in order to cover themselves against this contingency, in a land somewhat harassed by droughts, the priesthood developed the principle of human sacrifice, to appease and propitiate the gods and to prevail on them to send rain.

THE MAYAN ARMY

In addition to working in his own fields and in those of his religious and secular superiors, and to performing all the constructional tasks required of him the Mayan peasant was also expected to turn out to fight in the army. The organization of the army and its mode of campaign is discussed at greater length in the next chapter. Here it is sufficient to note that war was for the peasant a seasonal occupation. He engaged in it at times when he was not busy on the farm, notably in the dry season which began at the end of October. Every man capable of bearing arms was called out for the levy, and the women went along to prepare the food. Campaigns were short, though sharp, and were always brought to a close before the maize-planting season began—nothing was allowed to interfere with the all-important routine of agriculture.

In fighting the Mayan armies, the Spanish conquistadores discovered that they were up against a disciplined force, capable of quite intricate manoeuvres on the field of battle. Such perfection is not achieved without a great deal of training and practice, and it would seem likely that Mayan peasants devoted considerable time to military exercises. Discipline, however, was inherent in the Indian nations of America. The individual existed as a member of a tribe or clan, apart from which he had little significance. From the very beginning he learned to take his place as a member of a team. Group labour was the rule, whether in working the land or making roads or building pyramids or training for war.

We know little about the education of Mayan children. However, since the knowledge of reading, writing and figures was confined to an initiated caste, it can be assumed that education consisted chiefly of preparing children for their role in later life by subjecting them to discipline (as happened with the Aztecs) and training them in teamwork and the various skills they would need to acquire. Boys accompanied their fathers to the fields and were taught by them. They slept, however, in a communal dormitory until the time came for marriage. Girls were likewise instructed by their mothers. Above all, Mayan children had instilled into them the habit of instant and unquestioning obedience. They early became aware of their place in society and learned how to treat lords and other important people with due deference. The Maya were a malleable people.

BIRTH, MARRIAGE AND DEATH

Marriage among the Maya occurred at an early age—generally at about 18 for boys, 14 for girls. Soon after the celebration of puberty—at about 14 for boys, 12 for girls—the parents began to think about arranging partners for their children. As we have seen on page 67, their choice was restricted by taboos on marriage with persons of the same surname. Since, according to the early Spanish chroniclers, there were only about 250 patrilinear families in the whole of Yucatan at the time of the conquest, the limits must at times have been somewhat frustrating.

As with most important ceremonies among the Maya, the puberty celebrations were preceded by a period (three days in this instance) of fasting and sexual abstinence by the parents and other participants. Predictably they were communal occasions, with the parents of all the children concerned combining to meet the expense. In two parties, one of boys and one of girls, they assembled in a chosen courtyard—a local temple courtyard, according to some authors, the godfather's courtyard, according to others. There, on a carpet of leaves, sat four elders of the clan, one at each corner of a square, holding ropes which enclosed the square. Within it stood the children, facing a priest who squatted crosslegged beside a brazier.

Each child advanced in turn to stand before the priest, who, from two plates near at hand, gave the child a handful of ground maize and a pinch of copal. These the child had to throw into the brazier. Then, according to some versions, the child was invited to confess its sins, the very act of confession conferring absolution. The priest recited a lecture on the duties of maturity and the elders, who were holding the ropes, admonished them at length on the same theme. After this each child was anointed by the priest with pure water, and the tokens of childhood ceremoniously removed. These were a white bead which had been stuck to the top of the boy's head at birth, and a little shell suspended around the girl's middle, also at birth.

The ceremony at last complete, the priest handed the brazier and the ropes to an attendant who hastily carried them to the outskirts of the village and deposited them there. The Maya believed that with these objects he carried away any demons that had been exorcized from the children. The courtyard was swept clean of leaves and covered with a mat, so that any demons who did find their way back would not recognize the place. The celebration ended, as might be expected, with a feast.

Thereafter the parents of the children began to think of matrimony. To achieve a propitious union they engaged the services of a professional matchmaker, or *at atanzahob*. The matchmaker had not only to determine who were eligible to be marriage partners but also to investigate all the complex astrological implications. The respective horoscopes of the boy and girl had to be examined, to make sure that they were compatible, and an auspicious day for the wedding had to be carefully selected. The bride's parents did rather well out of the transaction. They received from the bridegroom's father a dowry, chiefly of clothes, and they also had their son-in-law to live with them and help with the work of the household for anything between five and seven years after the marriage. The young couple lived in a flimsy hut in the bride's father's compound.

On the day selected as propitious for the ceremony, both families assembled in the house of the bride's parents. There the priest said prayers over the bride and groom and blessed them. He also recited the conditions of the marriage, with special reference to the sums involved and the length of time the bridegroom had to work for his father-in-law. Gifts were exchanged, and everyone settled down to a feast and a carousal. Next day work went on as usual; there was no honeymoon for the newly-weds.

Among the Maya marriage was certainly instituted for the procreation of children. They liked large families. The attitude was perhaps instinctive, for the child mortality rate seems to have been high, and the wastage in adult life was also considerable. Twenty miles off the east coast of Yucatan the island of Cozumel held a shrine of the moon goddess, Ixchel, who was also the goddess of pregnancy; pregnant women would often make the pilgrimage, by dug-out canoe, to the island to ask for aid in childbirth. Barren women also made the trip, with prayers and offerings for fertility. It seems that the Maya believed that sexual intercourse was not only permissible but necessary during pregnancy, on the grounds that the woman needed a regular supply of the man's seminal fluid in order to make the baby. They also thought that the time of the child's conception had considerable influence on its future life. Certain unlucky days were to be avoided. The child's horoscope was prepared by priests who took into account the date of conception as well as that of birth.

The British archaeologist Eric S. Thompson quotes a seventeenth-century chronicler on an interesting Mayan birth ceremony:

To the accompaniment of prayers for his well-being, the child's umbilical cord was cut over a multi-coloured ear of maize with a brand new obsidian knife (thrown into the river after the ceremony). The blood-stained ear was smoke-cured, and at the appropriate season the grain was removed and sown with the utmost care in the name of the child. The yield was harvested and again sown, and the increased yield served, after a share had been given to the temple priest, to maintain the boy until he was old enough to sow his own *milpa*. They said that thereby he not only ate the sweat of his brow but of his own blood.

Within a few days of birth the child was strapped to the frame which, as we have seen on page 30, was to shape its head into the fashionable flattened form. From the frame a ball of resin was made to dangle just above the child's eyes in order to make it squint, another fashionable attribute. In infancy, too, the lobes of the ears, the nose and the lips were pierced, for the later insertion of ornaments.

Vogt describes present-day birth customs in Zinacantan. The mother is attended by the midwife and also by her husband and a number of her husband's relations. During and after the labour all, except the mother, refresh themselves with rum. The umbilical cord (severed with the point of a heated machete) and the afterbirth are buried in a rag in the patio. Immediately after cleaning the baby with a dry rag, the midwife washes the mother's hair.

Soon after birth the child is introduced to the tools it will use in later life. A boy is made to clench his fist on a dibbing-stick, a hoe, a billhook and other tools; a girl is given a *mano* for grinding maize, and the parts of a loom. At intervals of two days after the birth the mother has three sweat-baths. She is joined in the bath by the midwife, who rubs her down with myrtle and laurel leaves. Apart from that, however, for four or five days after the birth, no-one is supposed to pay any attention to either mother or baby. This is in order, presumably, not to draw the attention of evil spirits to the new baby. Similarly, the mother ties cords around the baby's wrists and ankles to prevent the escape of its soul.

Among the Classic Maya a ceremony, similar to that employed today by the Zinacantecos, was used to introduce a child to its future activities. The offering of the various tools and other objects was performed by the child's 'godfather'. There were nine objects, placed on a table. The godfather, with the baby on his hip, circled the table nine times, offering the child one of the objects at each perambulation. A godmother performed the same service for a girl baby.

At an appropriate time the baby was named. A lucky day for the ceremony had to be carefully chosen by the priest, for names were of supreme importance, indeed of magic potency. Every Maya had four names. One was his private name, given to him at the naming ceremony and corresponding to our Christian name. The second was his father's family name. Then came his mother's family name or, perhaps more frequently, a combination of the names of both his father's and his mother's families. Finally, he was given a nickname, by which he was generally known. This name became worn threadbare with use; the private name, on the other hand, retained its pristine power, being known to only a few people and very seldom used. Private names began with 'Ah' when masculine, and 'Ix' when feminine. At the time of marriage a new name was taken, comprising elements of both husband's and wife's names.

Death held terrors for the Maya. They regarded it as an escape of the soul from its familiar environment into—who knows what? There were numerous heavens and hells prepared for it, but the exact state of the soul in them was obscure. The Maya, like most primitive people, clung closely to what was known rather than adventuring into the unknown. Bishop de Landa, the first Christian bishop to minister in Yucatan, described their 'great and excessive fear of death; all the services performed for their gods were for no other purpose than that they should give them health and life . . . when death occurred they wept the day in silence, and at night they wailed.' According to von Hagen, the Maya regarded death as an anti-social act, a form of social defilement. This can perhaps best be appreciated by remembering the close social structure of the Maya. Almost every activity was a communal one. Death therefore deprived the clan of an able-bodied member, and those who were left had to take over his share of the work.

A dying man would confess to a priest, thus helping to dispel the demonic influences associated with death. A taboo was placed on the dead man's tools and other possessions, and these were either buried with him or destroyed. Before burial the corpse had a bead of jade or something similar placed in its mouth, as money for use in the next world. Pots filled with food

48 *The Maya were much concerned with death. The wall of this small building at Chichen Itza is entirely covered with a sculptured pattern of skulls.*

and drink were also placed in the grave. No doubt compassion for the dead by relatives who wanted to ensure that he would lack nothing in his new life was a powerful motive, but so also was the desire to provide the deceased with all he could need so that he would not come wandering back to haunt the living.

The funeral arrangements for a nobleman were more elaborate, for the simple reason that he had more possessions. Buried with him would be his jewels and ornaments, rich clothing, his weapons, his tableware, plenty of food, his favourite dog and, finally, a retinue of slaves, all with the tools of their respective crafts, so that they could continue to serve their master in the future life as they had served him on earth.

Nobles were often cremated, but ordinary people were more usually interred beneath the floors of their huts. After a number of burials had been made there, the huts were abandoned as dwelling-places and regarded as family shrines.

In the next world the dead would find no compensation for

privations in this. They were not rewarded or punished according to the kind of life they had led. Rather, they continued with the same sort of life. A peasant continued to work as a peasant, a noble remained a noble, and a slave, a slave.

MEDICINE

Primitive people commonly regard disease and illness as unnatural. A man may fall sick (1) through the inscrutable will of the gods, (2) as a punishment for past sins, perhaps in a previous incarnation, or (3) because he has been bewitched or ill-wished by an enemy. Whatever the reason, it is a matter for enlisting, if possible, the goodwill and cooperation of the gods. It was not otherwise with the Maya. Believing that illness was caused by supernatural forces, their reaction on falling sick was to call in the priest to do battle with them. The first thing the priest had to do was to determine who or what was responsible for the malady. This he did by divination, which involved the throwing of dice or of small bones, the burning of incense and the consultation of auguries. Treatment consisted of invocations to the appropriate god or goddess, the offering of sacrifices, and the administration of an ingenious variety of medicines.

The Maya evidently had a good working knowledge of the properties of many herbs, though any books on the subject which may once have existed have been lost. They put much store on tobacco, regarding it almost as a cure-all. Chroniclers of the Spanish period quote it as being used against such varied ills as toothache, snake-bite, asthma, indigestion, boils, headaches, catarrh and ailments associated with childbirth. It was also employed in divination and for warding off the evil eye. Other herbal remedies included a spurge-like plant (euphorbia), guavas, the sap of the rubber tree, and certain fungi, but with these the medicine-men mixed such revolting ingredients as boiled tapir dung, a whole bat dissolved in a fermented drink, a live toad likewise incorporated into a brew, woodpeckers' bills, feathers and the shredded testicles of a cock. One recipe recommended: 'If all else fails, have him remove one sandal, urinate in it and drink it.' Bleeding was also a common remedy.

Ixchel, the goddess of the moon and of pregnancy, was also the goddess of disease, thus indicating a belief, prevalent in many parts of the world, that there is a connection between certain ailments and the phases of the moon. We have already noted how pregnant women made pilgrimages to her shrine to seek help in childbirth. Bishop de Landa recorded how 'the doctors and shamans and their wives gathered in the house of one of their number, where the priests, after driving out the devil, brought out their medicine bundles in which they carried round many trifles and various little idols of the goddess of medicine Ix Chel.'

The sun-god, Ah Kin or Kinich Ahau, also had power over some diseases. Peasants used to pray to him for good health so that they could perform their daily labour in the sunlight. It was likewise worth invoking the aid of the fire-god, Kaak, and of the rain-gods, the latter, with some logic, being regarded as the senders of fever. There was also a god of herbal medicines, Ah Uincir Dz'acar.

The diseases from which the Maya suffered included pneumonia, pleurisy, rheumatism, some fevers, epilepsy, indigestion, toothache, sundry stomach worms, cancer, dysentery, erysipelas and jaundice. Opinions differ on whether yellow fever and perhaps malaria were present before the Spanish conquest. Certainly the Europeans imported such deadly maladies as syphilis, smallpox, measles and influenza, all of which took a heavy toll of the Indian population.

CRIME

Wrongdoing and disease are closely connected in the minds of many primitive peoples. Sickness, of course, is often thought to be the consequence of wrongdoing, but, more, sickness and crime are also often considered to derive from the same source. The reasoning is that both the man who is shivering from malaria and the man who has murdered his neighbour with an axe are more to be pitied than blamed, for both are equally under the influence of a malignant spirit.

Although the Maya had progressed beyond this way of thinking, at least to the extent of punishing crime according to a strict legal code, they were surprisingly lenient to certain types of wrongdoer. The unpardonable crimes were those against society, and particularly against the society formed by one's own group or clan. We have seen, for instance, that Mayan village houses not only had no locks, they had not even doors. Anyone could enter. Burglary therefore was an offence against one's own kin and was considered disgraceful. The thief had to make restitution. He had either to restore the stolen goods to the owner or to pay for them.

If he could not pay, he had to work for his victim until the debt was paid off; he became, in fact, a temporary slave. If he offended again, he was put to death.

Death, as we have seen, was regarded as a kind of disaster, both for the person concerned and for the group of which he was a member. Anyone therefore causing a person's death committed an offence against the whole clan. Here the primitive reasoning outlined above did apply: a man who killed another was obviously under the influence of an evil spirit who wished ill to the clan; it was therefore wiser to eliminate him. Whether the killing was deliberate or accidental made no difference. The evil spirit who caused the death certainly intended it, whether or not it was in the mind of the man whose hand committed the crime. Similarly no differentiation was made between accident and intent where property was concerned. If a man broke another's hoe or storage pot, he had to buy another to replace it.

Adultery was regarded as a serious crime. There was probably an element of damage to property in the reasoning which so condemned it. The aggrieved husband had a right to kill the wife's lover by dropping a rock on his head. It is not known whether a wife had a similar right if her husband transgressed, but probably not. Among the Quiche Maya it seems that a wife was sometimes punished as well as her husband if the husband committed adultery, on the grounds that if she had kept him content at home he would not have offended. These highland Maya also believed that the spirits of their ancestors watched over them and tried to stop them from committing crimes.

When in the tenth century Yucatan was invaded by the warlike Itza and their Mexican allies, the resident Maya were outraged not so much by the carnage and cruelties of the conquest but by the more intangible consequences of the debased code of conduct introduced by the newcomers. The Mayan *Book of Chilam Balam of Chumayel* (as translated by R. L. Roys in 1933) records how 'they [the invaders] brought shameful things when they came. They lost their innocence in carnal sin . . . This was the cause of our sickness also. There were no more lucky days for us; we had no sound judgment. At the end of our loss of vision and of our shame everything shall be revealed.' Here we can see the association of carnal sin with physical sickness, ill-luck and unbalanced judgment. Once order, discipline and correct social behaviour had been abandoned, the Maya believed, all sorts of ills could be expected as a matter of course.

6

Government and politics

At the head of the Mayan state sat the *halach uinic*, whose office was spiritual as well as temporal. He was, indeed, a kind of demi-god and was treated with exaggerated reverence by his subjects. The office was hereditary, generally passing down from father to the eldest son but sometimes to other members of the royal family. If the line failed, a new *halach uinic* could be elected by the council of state, which also appointed a regent in the event of the succession of a minor. The council of state seems to have been mainly an advisory body, with the *halach uinic* making the final decisions. To what extent he could be overridden in an emergency is uncertain. Among the members of the council were

49 *The head of a Mayan state was the* halach uinic, *a hereditary chief who presided over a council of state. This plaque from Piedras Negras shows a reconstruction of a council meeting.*

the chiefs, the *batab* (plural *batabob*) or administrators mentioned earlier, the more important priests and other persons of rank. It seems likely that most of them were related to the *halach uinic*, for they were appointed to the council by him, not elected.

In discussing Mayan politics and society it must be remembered that we are not dealing with a static situation but one which changed and developed over 1,000 or 1,500 years prior to the Spanish conquest. We naturally know more about the later part of the period than the earlier. By this time the Classic period of the Maya was over and they had fallen under foreign domination. As we have seen, the rule of the alien dynasty in Mayapan was so oppressive that in 1441 its Mayan subjects rose in revolt and destroyed it. Thereafter Yucatan disintegrated into a number of squabbling petty states, each under its own ruler, who seems often to have been a tyrant. For the period for which we have most information, therefore, the Mayan states were under the control of alien and resented rulers, who upheld their authority by force and relied for their revenue on taxes from an unwilling people. In such circumstances, the *halach uinic* would tend to surround himself with his own family, who had a strong vested interest in maintaining their dominant status. He would be the head of a closely-welded ruling clique, motivated by self-preservation. In the golden age of the Mayan civilization, 700 or 800 years earlier, things were probably very different.

The *batab* was an extremely important member of the council of state and was based in the capital. However, he was also supposed to undertake periodic rounds of the province under his control. On these visitations he was met with almost royal honours, sitting to dispense justice, accept tribute and generally oversee the affairs of the region. The day-to-day affairs of the cities were managed by a local council, composed of old and wise men—elders would be an appropriate term—who annually elected one of their number as chairman. The administration was thus on a par with the mayor and corporation of a European town.

While the council represented the civil government, military affairs were organized separately. They were under the authority of an officer, the *nacom*, who was elected or appointed (probably the latter) for a three-year term of office. There was also, however, a *nacom* who officiated at sacrifices. He was the man who, as in Aztec Mexico, slashed the breast of the victim and tore

50 *In this detail from a Bonampak mural, a Mayan band is playing in honour of a victorious chief.*

out his heart. It seems likely that the same name was used for two entirely distinct officers, though it is possible that the two offices were combined in the same person.

There is some confusion about the nature of the Mayan army which the *nacom* commanded. As already mentioned, the discipline they exhibited in the field indicated a highly trained force. There must have been a great deal of drilling and exercises, but there was, however, no standing army. Except during an actual campaign the soldiers stayed at home and worked on their farms. Only when they were on active service were they paid for their military duties. It is said that every able-bodied man was liable for military service, but there are other references to the soldier as a figure of some respect. Evidently there was a kind of local militia, whether raised by voluntary service or by conscription, which was commanded by an official known as the *al holpop*. When required, the *al holpop* and his contingent would report to the *nacom*. There seem also, at least in later times, to have been bands of full-time mercenaries, known as *holkans*, under the command of permanent leaders.

WARFARE

The fact that most of the Mayan cities of the Classic period were undefended by walls or moats indicates that regular war then was rare. Such engagements as are depicted on murals are more in the nature of raids than all-out war. In later times the situation deteriorated, and the squabbling city-states into which Yucatan split after the fall of Mayapan were almost constantly at war. One Spanish chronicler remarked: 'They never knew peace, especially when the corn harvest was over.'

Even war, however, was, before the Spanish conquest, a phenomenon of very limited duration. A battle always ended at nightfall, when the combatants retired to eat the supper their womenfolk had been preparing for them. Nor could a campaign be conducted far from home, for not only did the women and slaves have to carry on their backs the provisions for the army but everyone had to be prepared to pack up and go home when they were needed on the farm. In their later wars against the Spaniards the Maya were usually handicapped by this concept of warfare: they were a peasant militia, bred to giving priority to things of the soil, matched against a professional, full-time army. The people of western Europe were hampered by exactly the same impediment in the ninth and tenth centuries in their wars against the Danes and Vikings.

In one other respect, the Mayan ideas on war differed radically from those of Europeans. For the Maya, the prime purpose of war was to capture, not to kill, the enemy. In particular, they wanted to capture the *nacom*, the enemy leader. Once he was seen to be taken, the battle was over. His army melted away, leaving him to be carried in triumph to his captors' city, there to be offered in ceremonial sacrifice. The same fate befell his officers and other persons of rank. Ordinary soldiers and their followers were enslaved.

A short, vigorous campaign as favoured by the Maya could best be achieved by a surprise attack. In organizing this the Maya were adept. They prepared the ground well, with the aid of an efficient scouting service. Then, assembling in ambush, they suddenly charged, with a maximum of wild warcries, trumpets blowing, drums beating and whistles piping. The *nacom* and his subordinates were gorgeously arrayed, in magnificent feathered headdresses that greatly increased their apparent height, and wearing flashing jewellery. A Mayan onslaught must have been a

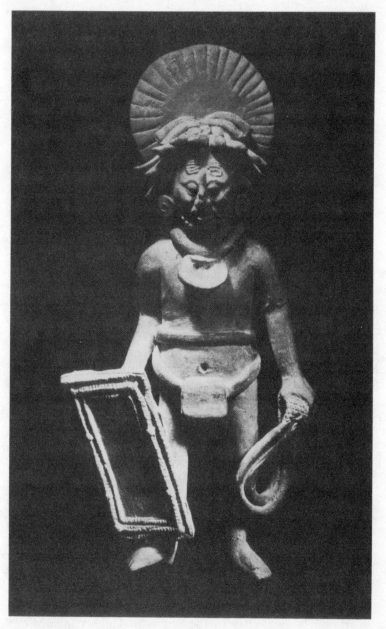

51 *A terracotta warrior from Jaina, carrying a shield and a sling.*

52 *A clay whistle from Jaina in the shape of a warrior carrying a large shield and club. The whistle itself provides an interesting example of a Mayan musical instrument.*

terrifying experience for an unprepared enemy.

The original Mayan weapons were the lance, the club, the dagger and a kind of trident made by carving three sharp blades from a large seashell. These last two were used for hand-to-hand fighting. The Mexican invaders of the ninth century introduced the bow and arrow, and also a spear-throwing device known as the *atl-atl* which enabled spears to be hurled in rapid succession. It gave them a critical advantage in the type of warfare to which the Maya were accustomed. The standard procedure was for an exchange of missiles, both spears and sling-stones, followed by a closing in for hand-to-hand combat. With their arrows and *atl-atl* the Mexicans were able to prolong the long-distance fighting until the battle was virtually won. Probably as an answer to these new tactics, the Maya manufactured a kind of quilted armour by soaking a padded cotton tunic in salt brine. They also enlarged the size of their shields.

During the centuries of Mexican domination the invaders became an unpopular aristocracy. Under such circumstances it was natural for the young nobles, who considered themselves above manual work, to form warrior societies which were, in operation, very similar to the orders of knights in medieval Europe. Chief of these were several orders of the Jaguar and the Eagle. Though primarily military orders, they had close religious associations, much as did the medieval Templars. Murals depict knights of the Order of Jaguars sacrificing a victim, in the accepted Mayan manner, and others show them engaging in a sacrificial dance. In this latter ceremony the knights 'fought' with a captive who was tied to a stake and had only a wooden sword decorated with feathers with which to defend himself. When he had worn himself out the captive was killed and skinned, and his skin worn by one of the dancers.

THE PRIESTHOOD

The priests formed a numerous sector in Mayan society. As in most civilizations there was a strict priestly hierarchy, with at the head the high priests, or *Ah Kin*. Beneath them came both assistant and specialist priests. The latter included the *nacom*, already mentioned, who conducted sacrifices; the *chilan*, who was a kind of medium or soothsayer; and the *chac*, an elder who assisted at the sacrifices. The functions of the priesthood were many. The accumulated knowledge of the Maya was invested in their priests, who alone held the key to the Mayan glyphs and counting system. Not only did the priests preside over sacrifices, the chief purpose of which was to satisfy the gods, they also read and interpreted the omens in the sacrifices. Because of the need to prepare horoscopes by astrology, they became competent astronomers. Perhaps most important of all, they devised a remarkably detailed almanac, from which they retailed to the laity information about religious celebrations, the dates to plant crops, the imminence of eclipses and similar details. Perpetuating such knowledge must have involved the establishment of schools, which would have been run by the priests, but little is known of them.

The priesthood was partly hereditary. Many, perhaps most, priests were the sons of priests. Some, however, were recruited from the younger sons of the nobility. And, as we have already noted, the *halach uinic* combined a few religious and sacerdotal functions with his secular authority. So, although the Mayan states were controlled by the dual authority of priests and nobles, there was no fundamental conflict between the two: they were all related. Priests and nobles formed a closely-knit community based on their city houses around the temple pyramids. Religious observances in the villages were in the hands of local priests, who seem mainly to have been concerned with divination, though

53 *A jaguar throne from Chichen Itza, which was used by a* halach uinic *or other notability. It was painted red and inlaid with jade and shells.*

that term covers a great deal—from the determining of lucky days for weddings to the diagnosis of sickness, the requirements of the gods in the matter of sacrifice, and the uncovering of witchcraft.

The *chacs* were laymen, though elderly men of acknowledged respectability and knowledge. We have seen (page 71) how they held the four corners of the rope square in which adolescents were confined during the puberty ceremony. Four chacs also held the four limbs of a victim being sacrificed. According to Bishop de Landa, the *chacs* included among their number workmen skilled in woodcarving, who were on occasion shut up in strict seclusion to make wooden idols of the gods. So although there were *chacs* in the sacred precincts of the city temples, they were also present in the countryside, at hand to help with local ceremonies, thus representing one sphere in which the priesthood kept contact with ordinary people.

The *chilan* was another priestly character who circulated among the masses. Predictably, because he was able to interpret the will of the gods, he was treated with some reverence and was carried

54 *Here, from a lintel of a house in Yaxchilan, is a scene depicting a penitent kneeling before a priest and mutilating his tongue by drawing a rope studded with thorns through it.*

55 *Man offering a sacrifice, a terracotta figurine from Jaina. The attitude of the Maya to their gods was one of immense respect.*

about on a litter. When preparing to prophesy he underwent a period of ritual purification which included prolonged fasting and continence. Mayan texts, if their translation is correct, indicate that his seances took place in a hut, in which the *chilan*, in a trance, prostrated himself on the floor and received messages from the god in the rafters. It seems likely that narcotics were used to help the *chilan* into a trance.

Below the *chacs* and *chilans* came a humbler order of acolytes known as '*ah men*'. Their role was to ensure that the gods' instructions (relayed through the priests) were translated into action in the everyday life of the farm. They conducted certain ceremonies involving divination and the cure of the sick and were also regarded as prayermakers, who, apparently for a fee, would address a prayer to a god.

The attitude of the Mayan peasant to the gods was one of immense respect, even fear. He was anxious not to put a foot wrong, for fear of the consequences. His prayers were therefore either requests for favours or thanksgiving for past benefits. There was little morality in them. On the other hand, every Mayan peasant felt an identity with the crops he grew and the creatures with which he shared this world. The life of the maize and his own life were inextricably entwined. Likewise every animal in the forest had a soul, which was protected by the gods of the earth. A man could kill an animal if he needed to, but before or immediately afterwards he had to offer an apology. To ward off possible retribution he would sometimes hand over his booty to friends and then accept part of it back again. He could thus claim that he was eating only what had been given to him.

The city of Uxmal includes a building that has become known as 'the Nunnery', because of the tradition that it once housed girls who were the equivalent of vestal virgins. The British expert Eric S. Thompson considers that this is unlikely. The Maya, however, did have a religious order of celibate women, whose duties included elaborate embroidery in textiles and feathers, cleaning of the temples and tending the sacred fires.

7

Gods and Goddesses

The Mayan pantheon was very complex, and unravelling it is
made none the easier by the fact that our information is
incomplete, despite one record dating from the Spanish conquest
which contains the names of 166 gods. Many of these were
probably imported by the Mexicans. It is therefore difficult to
find out exactly what was the state of Mayan thinking in the
Classic period.

The Maya believed that the Otherworld consisted of layers,
arranged horizontally. Thirteen of these were in the sky and were
roughly equivalent to Heaven; nine were beneath the earth and
represented Hell. Heaven and Hell, however, were not considered either as reward or punishment for behaviour on earth.
Rather they were the after-life abodes natural to different classes
of people: one passed on to the sphere appropriate to one's class
and occupation.

Just as four *chacs* acted as pillars of the rope square enclosing
the boys and girls at the puberty ceremony, and just as four *chacs*
held the four limbs of the victim on the stone of sacrifice, so four
gods, called *Bacabs*, held the heavens up on their shoulders—like
Atlas quadrupled. Each *Bacab* was associated with a direction
and with a colour. The one on the northern side was white; the
one on the west, black; the one on the south, yellow; and the one
on the east, red. Near each *Bacab* grew a tree of the corresponding
colour (though it may be that the *Bacabs* themselves were thought
of as taking the form of trees). In the centre was a fifth tree,
coloured green, and each tree held a bird of the appropriate
colour.

90

56 *Mayan gods tended to have four aspects. This figurine may*
represent the four Bacabs *who upheld the world on their shoulders.*

The Maya conceived the idea of a supreme god, and his name
was Hunab Ku, but he was so remote, impersonal and incom-
prehensible that in practice little account was taken of him. His
son, Itzamna, was the god of the heavens and of night and day.
He was the donor to mankind of food, medicine, the art of writing
and many other gifts. In Mayan art he is depicted as an old man
with a lizard's body, the lizard being his sign. He is cross-eyed
and toothless and often wears a beard. The thinking about
Itzamna tends to be somewhat obscure, largely because, by his
very omnipotence, he was beyond the grasp of ordinary people,

57 right *A limestone figure of the maize-god from Copan. Maize was very important to the Maya, and much of their worship centred on it.*

58 below *Rain was also important for the Maya. Here, from a design incised on a bone from a temple at Tikal, are three rain-gods catching fish. Note the eager expressions on their faces. Not all Mayan art was always serious.*

who preferred the more specialized and compartmentalized deities, of which they had an immense range.

Each of the zones of Heaven and Hell had its own god. The names of some of them have not yet been deciphered, but it is known that each of the gods of the Underworld presided over one of the days of the Mayan calendar. On a larger time-scale, each of the katun, or periods of 20 years, into which the Maya divided time, was under the patronage of a god, and since there were 13 katun it may perhaps be assumed that the gods of each of the layers of Heaven had rights over one katun.

In addition to the gods of the Otherworld, a vast array of gods controlled men's activities on earth. Among the more important were the rain-god, the maize-god, the war-god, the god of medicine, the wind-god, the god of death, the moon-goddess, the sun-god, the god of the North Star and sundry gods of the earth, including the jaguar-god. This situation was complicated by the fact that each god had both a good and an evil aspect. The rain-god, for example, brought water for the crops and to replenish the springs, which was good; but he also brought floods and consequent disease, which was bad. Similarly, the sun-god was both beneficent, in providing warmth and light, and malevolent, in producing drought and thirst. Each god in the Maya pantheon had a dual personality. A further complication arose because each god possessed both male and female attributes, and because each had one set of characteristics in Heaven and another in Hell. Thus the sun-god descended at sunset into the realms beneath the earth, there to become the jaguar-god.

According to one version of Mayan theology, Itzamna was the father of all the other gods (except Hunab Ku). His consort was Ixchel, who was thus the mother of all the other gods. She was the goddess not only of the moon but of pregnancy, of floods, and of weaving and other domestic arts. Nevertheless there seems to have been another moon-goddess, Ixchup, distinguished by some authorities as the 'Young Moon Goddess', who was the wife of a sun-god named Ah Kinchil. Were Ixchup and Ah Kinchil simply aspects of Ixchel and Itzamna respectively, or were they distinct deities? Who can say? Perhaps even the Maya were not clear on the question. Consider, after all, the controversies that have raged around the Christian doctrine of the Trinity.

REGIONAL VARIATIONS

When confronted with the multiplicity of Mayan gods, it is worth remembering that many names on the impressive list may be synonyms for the same god rather than references to completely different entities. The theology varies from region to region of the Mayan territory. The attempted summary above deals with lowland Yucatan. The Chorti people, who are Maya living in eastern Guatemala and adjacent districts, replace the *Bacabs* with *Chiccans*, who are gigantic snakes. There are four *Chiccans*, each one living in vast lakes which are situated at the four cardinal points of the compass. Each one is associated with a colour (as are the *Bacabs*), and also with certain days.

There are minor *Chiccans* past number. Thompson says that

59 *These serpent columns at the approach to the Temple of the Warriors at Chichen Itza are a reminder that giant snakes feature in many aspects of Mayan worship.*

they live 'in streams, springs and lakes, but as the dry season approaches they travel upstream and, entering springs, live during the dry season in the hills from which the springs issue. At the start of the rains, the *Chiccans* re-enter the streams, the size of their bodies causing the waters to swell; if too many swim downstream at one time, the river overflows its banks. Movements of *Chiccans* within the hills cause earthquakes; a tremor indicates the *Chiccan* is turning over in his sleep, and a violent earthquake ensues if the *Chiccan* turns completely over to lie on his other side.'

The Maya of Yucatan had a similar god, Mam, who caused earthquakes in the same way. To them too belonged a multiplicity of minor gods, many of them important because they had authority in important facets of everyday life. There were gods of the various crops, of animals, of various trades and crafts; gods of rivers, lakes and caves; gods of the winds that blow from the several points of the compass. The duality attached to certain gods sometimes strikes us as surprising. For instance, the god of war, Ek Chuah, was also the beneficent god of merchants. The chief *Bacab*, whose name was Hobnil, was also the bee-god, or the patron god of beekeepers. Here again we encounter plurality, for there were several gods of both bees and merchants. Ek Chuah,

60 *The god of the cocoa-bean, from Guatemala. This figure is also a flute.*

61 *The Dresden Codex is concerned mainly with the rotations of the planet Venus, and the Venus god was an important deity in the Mayan pantheon. This detail from the Codex shows the Venus god hurling a spear. The original drawing can be seen on the left.*

too, is the god of the cacao crop, perhaps because cocoa-beans were a form of currency used by merchants.

Among the more obscure gods were those of tattooing, of sharks, of the chachalaca bird, of the makers of *balche* (wine), of deer and of ball-game players. Animals and other creatures had their own gods, who had to be treated by humans with respect. Besides these homely deities there were others of interest almost exclusively to the priestly hierarchy. Such were the star gods, as of Venus and the Pole Star. The Venus god or goddess seems to have had an additional earthly role as the patron of hunters, and was also associated with one of the Mayan months.

CHRISTIANITY

The process of reconciling their ancient religious beliefs with the Christianity introduced by their Spanish conquerors presented no great difficulties to the Mayan mind. Their religion today is a form of Christianity into which very many of their tenets have been absorbed—it is, in fact, an amalgam of Christianity and traditional Mayan lore. The multitudinous Mayan gods have become Christian saints (as, indeed, happened in many European countries in the early days of Christianity), and the saints' days conveniently perpetuate age-old Mayan festivals.

More fundamentally, the Maya found they could readily comprehend the Christian sacrament of eating bread and drinking wine. The idea of Christ being the bread of life was not a new one to them; it was a role exactly replicated by their maize-god. And there are stranger analogies. In the New Testament Book of Revelation we read of the Four Horsemen of the Apocalypse, whose horses are white, black, red and pale. In Mayan mythology the four *Bacabs* who inhabit the four quarters of the sky also ride on horseback, and the colours associated with the four quarters are the same as those of the Biblical horses.

Just as the Mayan religion had to come to terms with Christianity, so in an earlier age it had to absorb new deities introduced by the Mexican conquerors. Chief among these was Quetzalcoatl (in the conquerors' language) or Kukulcan (in the Mayan), who seems to have been a Mexican leader afterwards deified. His sign was the feathered serpent, a favourite theme in much Mayan art. New gods of the sun and of fire were also introduced, as well as the horrid god of spring, Xipe Totec, whose effigy had to be clothed in the skins of sacrificial victims.

97

THE REPRESENTATION OF MAYAN GODS

The gods in Mayan art were represented in kaleidoscopic fashion, each god or goddess appearing sometimes in one form, sometimes in another. Certain conventions, however, make them frequently recognizable. Quetzalcoatl, or Kukulcan, was, as we have noted, generally depicted as a plumed serpent. Itzamna usually had the body of a lizard or iguana. His wife, Ixchel, although in general a beneficent diety, often took the form of an old woman in a bad temper. The 'Young Moon Goddess', Ixchup, was perhaps Ixchel in a more attractive guise. Yum Kaax, the maize-god, was always young and held in his hands a pot containing a leafy maize plant. His head was so moulded that it was elongated almost to a point, thus resembling the shape of the maize leaf in his pot. The *Chacs* had trunks like a tapir, or elephant, and prominent teeth. Ek Chuah, the god of the Underworld and of death, was a black, evil-looking personage, with a protruding lower lip. Ah Puch, another god of death, was depicted as a skeleton. His cloak was hung with bells, and he was attended by a dog, an owl and other birds of ill-omen.

One of the gods of Venus was always blindfolded. Another was apparently a puma; and another had a green-plumaged bird set in one ear. Ixchab, the goddess of suicide (an honourable action, incidentally, in the Mayan code and instrumental in gaining a sure and immediate access to Heaven), was depicted with a twisted rope around her neck. Hobnil, the chief of the *Bacabs*, was often drawn as a stylized bee. And the jaguar-god, with his jaguar mask, was always unmistakeable.

COMMUNICATING WITH THE GODS

With such a multiplicity of gods the ordinary Mayan peasant had his work cut out to keep them all pacified, especially since propitiation demanded not moral conduct but the correct ceremonies, rituals and sacrifices carried out at the proper times. Clearly the task was one to keep the numerous priesthood continually busy.

On a personal level, the Mayan peasant would offer prayer at the beginning of the day, before breakfast. He would present special supplications for specific needs, such as success in hunting, being careful not to ask for more than he really needed. If his prayer were granted, he would offer thanks with an appropriate sacrifice. Along the paths leading from the village were shrines at which a man could pray, and outside them piles of stones, or cairns, to which he would add a stone each time he made a petition.

A priest had to be called in to determine the auspicious day for important events such as a marriage or the puberty festival. He was likewise in demand in case of illness, which was another matter for proper representation to the appropriate gods. There was, in fact, very little that a Mayan could do without reference to the gods, usually through the intermediary of a priest.

Individuals, except those of the highest social order, were not of great importance in the Mayan state. The state itself, or society as a whole, was the essential unit, and the well-being of the state was the primary object of religious observance. The worship of

62 *This reclining stone figure from Chichen Itza is known as a* Chac Mool, *and was used for holding a bowl during the sacrifices.*

the gods was something of a commercial transaction: benefits could only be expected if the gods were properly paid, and the payment demanded for more important occasions was human sacrifice. To what extent the Mayan sacrifices were derived from the bloodthirsty Mexican practices, and to what extent they were in vogue before the Mexican invasion, we do not know. Certainly human sacrifice was not engaged in by the Maya on the same scale as by the Aztecs, who, a few years before the Spanish conquest, ritually slaughtered 20,000 captured soldiers in a single day. The method of sacrifice was, however, very similar. The victim, painted blue, was spread-eagled over a slaughter-stone, with four attendants (*chacs*) holding his four limbs. A priest, with a violent downward thrust, slashed his left breast below the ribs and, plunging in his hand, drew out the still throbbing heart. Another priest then presented the heart to the god to whom the sacrifice had been made, smearing the blood on his image.

A sacrifice could be made in a temple courtyard and, indeed, almost anywhere, but the usual venue was a platform on top of a temple pyramid. On such occasions, a common procedure was to roll the dead body down the steps of the pyramid. At the bottom it was flayed, and the skin donned by one of the priests, who then danced in it. Occasionally the body was ritually eaten, so that the qualities of the dead person could be absorbed by the partakers. There were variations on this procedure. Sometimes the victim was tied to a stake for the operation. Some friars who were captured by the last independent Maya, the Itza, in 1696, were tied to a frame of poles shaped like a St Andrew's cross. Sometimes the victim was thrown from the top of a pyramid or other high place before his heart was removed. An alternative method of slaughter was by arrow. The victim was tied to a stake, with the position of his heart marked by a white spot, as a target for the archers. The first arrows were, however, deliberately aimed at other parts of his body, including his genitals.

Sacrificial victims could be men, women, children or even animals, though the most frequent were enemies captured in war. While awaiting an auspicious day, the captives were often confined in cages, closely guarded to ensure that they did not escape. In general, the possibility of being requisitioned for sacrifice was a hazard that the Maya must have lived with all their lives. It is therefore quite likely that many of them came to their destiny if not willingly at least with resignation. It has also

63 *One of the murals at Bonampak. Prisoners of war are brought before the victorious chief and tortured. Blood is dripping from their fingers where their nails have been torn out. This picture can be seen in colour on the jacket.*

been suggested that they were often drugged, though this has not been proved. Sometimes the victim was even required to join in the ritual dance with his butchers.

The astonishing murals of Bonampak (see page 117) depict prisoners of war undergoing torture. Some have had their fingernails torn out and are ruefully surveying the blood dripping from their fingertips. Another is senseless with exhaustion. Nothing similar, however, has been found elsewhere. One other form of sacrifice was common among the Maya of Yucatan. It was practised in time of drought, to propitiate the rain-god (or gods). The rain-gods of Yucatan were believed to live in the *cenotes*—deep limestone caves from which the roof had broken

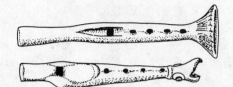

64 above *Mayan musical instruments : wooden flutes and a wooden drum.*

65 above *This drawing from the Madrid Codex shows a singing dog playing a gourd drum, another favourite Mayan musical instrument. The bubbles coming out from the dog's mouth represent his singing. Much of Mayan art uses this technique to indicate sound, particularly speech.*

away and which provided an important source of water for the lowland Maya. When drought prevailed, therefore, human victims were hurled into the *cenotes* from the surrounding cliffs, with instructions to plead with the gods below. The experience was generally fatal, but one hero survived, to become a famous chieftain. In addition to human sacrifice, all manner of other gifts were thrown into the *cenotes*.

RITUALS

Almost all Mayan ceremonies required due preparation. This involved fasting and abstention from sexual intercourse. Virginity was highly prized, which is thought to account for the great numbers of children sacrificed as 'pure' victims. 'Virgin' water, which was water collected from an underground spring or from drippings in a cave, was essential for most sacrifices. When fire was needed, it had to be 'virgin' fire—that is, fire created new by a priest twirling a stick in soft, tinder-like wood.

Dancing was an important feature of religious ritual, the purpose evidently being to produce an hypnotic effect on the participants, and also on the spectators. The dances were performed to the accompaniment of music. The Maya had a variety of wind and percussion instruments but no stringed ones. Wind instruments, such as flute or trumpet, carried the melody, while percussion intruments beat the time. A mural at Bonampak depicts an orchestra of 12 musicians. Two trumpeters led the procession, supported by drummers (one on a kettle-drum and three on drums made of turtle-shells) and players with rattles. The leader sang the tune and conducted the orchestra. Players who made a mistake in the rhythm were subject to punishment. This mural does not show all the instruments known to the Maya. They also employed flutes, pan-pipes and bells, the last being usually tied to the wrists, ankles and belts of dancers. Flutes were made of reed, ceramics and bones (sometimes human bones). The trumpets illustrated at Bonampak are ceramic but others were of wood. One of the commonest types of drum was a hollowed log with a deerskin stretched over it. It was played by striking with the hand, but others were beaten with sticks tipped with rubber. Large seashells were widely used both as drums and trumpets.

An early Spanish chronicle described a dance in Yucatan:

The Indians prepared a sort of float and placed on top of it a sort of narrow turret about six feet high and somewhat like a pulpit. This was covered from top to bottom with painted cotton cloths, and two flags were at the top, one on each side. A handsomely dressed Indian, visible from the waist up, was in this tower. He had a rattle of the kind they use in this land in one hand, and a feather fan in the other. All the time he kept shaking his body and whistling to the beating of an upright

66 *Mayan actors wore fantastic masks of animals, birds and reptiles.*
This wooden jaguar mask comes from the highlands of Guatemala.

drum which another Indian, alongside the float, was playing.
With him were many other Indians who sang to the same
drum, making a great row and giving many piercing whistles.
Six Indians carried the float on their shoulders, and even they
moved forward singing, dancing and wriggling their bodies to
the sound of the drum. That turret was very handsome, and
swayed a great deal, and one could see it from far off because of
its height and its bright colours. That dance was called Zono,
and is one of those they used in ancient times.

It could well be a description of a pop group in a present-day
town carnival. In another dance, the Colomche, or Dance of the

Reeds, Bishop de Landa records that 150 dancers, gyrating in a circle, took part. In the centre of the circle two dancers mimed the parts of a hunter and a deer (or perhaps a hunted man). De Landa was much impressed with the skill of the performance, as were the spectators, for he mentions that they numbered 15,000 and came from miles around. Yet another dance required 800 dancers, who kept up the action all day long, non-stop. This was apparently a war-dance. Most Mayan dances seem to have been decorous, and in general men and women did not participate in the same dance. The early Spanish friars, however, found a few of them indecent and erotic.

Many, perhaps most, Mayan dances had an element of drama, fitting in, as they did, with a ceremony in honour of a god from whom favours were hoped for. The demarcation line between such ceremonies and stage drama is blurred, but evidently dramatic art was fairly well developed, and talented actors found work to do. Murals depict actors wearing fantastic masks of animals, birds and reptiles, while others have stylized costumes, the meaning of which was no doubt clear to the audience. One is reminded of the mumming plays that still survive in parts of rural England in which the champions of light fight with and overcome the champions of darkness, or of the plays associated with the revival of nature, and hence with fertility, such as are still widely performed in many parts of Europe. As in most other examples of primitive drama, the Mayan plays included elements of light relief and humour. De Landa found Mayan actors extremely witty and excellent mimics.

The plays were performed in the open air, on platforms of stone constructed for the purpose. They were put on, says de Landa, 'for the pleasure of the public', and he terms some of them 'farces' and some 'comedies'. There may well have been tragedies, too, for one of these stages, at Chichen Itza, is decorated on all sides with rows of human skulls, carved in stone. This stage adjoins the ball court, where, as already mentioned, murals depict the winner of a ball game holding up the decapitated head of his defeated opponent. Dr Michael Coe has commented that 'it is entirely possible that the game was played "for keeps", the losers ending up on the Tzompantli [the stage]'. The association between dance, music, drama and games is thus shown to be close, and all are connected, in some degree, with religious ceremonies.

8

Mathematics, science and literature

Among the Maya mathematics and literature were esoteric arts: although many books existed, there was no general knowledge of reading and writing. Graffiti by workmen can sometimes be seen on the walls of Mayan buildings, but they take the form of pictures. Nor does writing appear to have been used for recording contracts or other commercial matters. Mathematics were employed, to a limited extent, by merchants, who, says de Landa, made calculations by means of counters, probably cocoa-beans, 'on the ground or on a flat surface'. The more advanced exercises of mathematics were, however, like the art of writing in Mayan glyphs, reserved for and jealously guarded by the priests.

The priests formed a numerous class, and as a result the volume of Mayan writing was quite considerable. When in 1562 Bishop de Landa issued a decree requiring all Mayan books to be surrendered and burned, they came in by hundreds. 'They contained nothing in which there was not to be seen superstitition and lies of the devil, so we burned them all,' wrote the Bishop. Later he bitterly regretted his fanatical action and tried to make some restitution, but, as far as is known, of all that literature only three books have survived.

In the absence of the original Mayan writings, it is on Bishop de Landa himself that we have to rely for much of our knowledge of the Maya of his time. In addition to a mass of information on their customs, beliefs, history and achievements, he has supplied us with a key of sorts to the Mayan hieroglyphic writing, without which its decipherment could not have progressed as far as it has. As it is, we are still only able to read about half of the Mayan glyphs, and these are the ones concerned with dates, astronomical matters and the calendar. The three original Mayan books still extant deal mainly with astronomy, astrology and ritual, while the books destroyed are thought to have ranged over a wide range of subjects, including history, genealogies, mythology (or religious treatises), medicine and divination. In addition to the surviving books, however, a further source of information is available in the numerous inscriptions on buildings and monuments. In keeping with the Mayan obsession with the calendar, these almost always give dates, which we can read, and proper names, which in most instances we cannot. Our knowledge of Mayan chronology, therefore, is reasonably exact and comprehensive from the Formative Period onwards, but much else is obscure.

MATHEMATICS

The Mayan system of numbers was brilliantly conceived and far superior in most respects to the system that served the Roman world for centuries. It made use of two concepts that are familiar to us but which we would find far from obvious if we had to start again from scratch: (1) associating value with position, and (2) the idea of zero.

If we write the figures 123 in that order we shall, because we have been initiated, read them as 'one hundred and twenty-three'. The figure on the right represents units, the one in the middle refers to the number of tens, and the one on the left the number of hundreds. We have, in effect, stated an arithmetical sum: we have added together one hundred, two tens and three units. Zero is important because it enables us to maintain the desired sequence under circumstances that would otherwise cause confusion. Supposing we want to write 'one hundred and three', we use the zero sign to keep the hundreds and the units apart. Without it we would just have to leave a gap between the one (hundred) and the three (units), which could be misunderstood.

The Maya used positioning and zero in exactly the same way. They, however, worked in vertical columns instead of horizontal ones. And they used not a decimal system, like ours, but a vigesimal one, or one based on twenties. The number of possible permutations was endless, and enabled the Maya to produce astronomical calculations. Indeed the very ease with which they could be accomplished seems to have tempted Mayan mathema-

THE MAYAN NUMBER SYSTEM

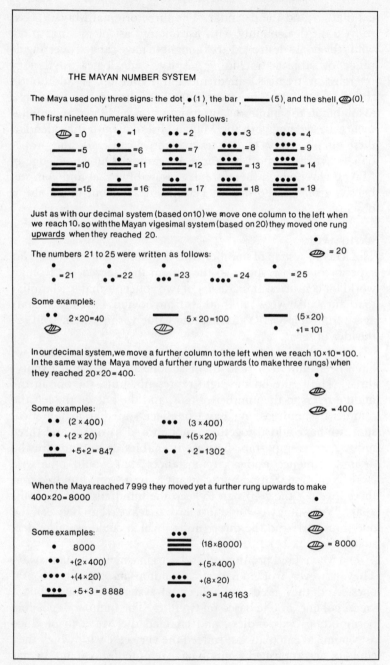

The Maya used only three signs: the dot, ● (1), the bar, ▬▬ (5), and the shell, 𝕮 (0).

The first nineteen numerals were written as follows:

𝕮 = 0   ● =1   ●● =2   ●●● =3   ●●●● =4
▬ =5   ▬●̇ =6   ▬●̇● =7   ▬●̇●● =8   ▬●̇●●● =9
═ =10   ═●̇ =11   ═●̇● =12   ═●̇●● =13   ═●̇●●● =14
☰ =15   ☰●̇ =16   ☰●̇● =17   ☰●̇●● =18   ☰●̇●●● =19

Just as with our decimal system (based on 10) we move one column to the left when we reach 10, so with the Mayan vigesimal system (based on 20) they moved one rung **upwards** when they reached 20.

The numbers 21 to 25 were written as follows:

● / 𝕮 = 20

● / ● =21   ● / ●● =22   ● / ●●● =23   ● / ●●●● =24   ● / ▬ =25

Some examples:

●● / 𝕮   2×20=40   ▬ / 𝕮   5×20=100   ▬ / ●   (5×20) +1 = 101

In our decimal system, we move a further column to the left when we reach 10×10=100. In the same way the Maya moved a further rung upwards (to make three rungs) when they reached 20×20=400.

● / 𝕮 / 𝕮 = 400

Some examples:

●● / ●● / ▬+●●   (2 × 400) +(2 × 20) +5+2 = 847

●●● / ▬ / ●●   (3 × 400) +(5 × 20) + 2 =1302

When the Maya reached 7999 they moved yet a further rung upwards to make 400×20=8000

● / 𝕮 / 𝕮 / 𝕮 = 8000

Some examples:

● 8000
●● +(2×400)
●●●● +(4×20)
●●● ▬ +5+3 = 8888

●●● / ═☰ / ▬ / ●●●   (18×8000) +(5×400) +(8×20) +3 = 146163

ticians into projections which can have little meaning. One inscription refers to a date of about four hundred million years ago, while an alautun was a period of time consisting of 23,040,000,000 days!

The Maya's mathematical prowess was chiefly used by their priests for the perfection of calendars. The word is advisedly used in the plural, for they had at least three.

One, called the *Haab* year, corresponded with our own. It consisted of 18 months, or *uinal*, of 20 days each. That made a total of 360 days, leaving 5 or $5\frac{1}{2}$ days over. These were known as *uayeb*, or unlucky days, and were devoted to religious ceremonies concerned with the New Year. The *Haab* year was also known as the Vague Year. The second calendar was concerned with the *Tzolkin* and was regarded as sacred. It consisted of 20 'months' of 13 days. The total of days was thus 260, a figure which bears no relationship to any natural calendar. How or why it originated is a mystery. Thirdly, there was the Long Count, a term which every reader of books on the Maya soon recognizes. It was an extension of the *Haab* calendar; starting with the unit of one *Haab* year of 360 days, termed a *tun*, it led back to a mystic year of 3113 B.C.

Looking at the three calendars in greater detail, it soon becomes obvious that they served the useful function of providing a check on each other. Every day had two labels, one in accordance with the *Haab* year, one with the *Tzolkin* year. Each day of the *Tzolkin* year coincided with the same day in the *Haab* year once every 18,980 days; 73 *Tzolkin* years equalled 52 *Haab* years, and at the end of 52 *Haab* years the cycle began again. The Maya were aware of this cycle and it held special meaning for them, particularly with regard to building pyramids. It was sometimes referred to as the Calendar Round.

The Maya also knew at least two other calendars, one of which was a lunar calendar. Eventually the Maya mathematicians achieved such accuracy that they were able to calculate the length of the lunar month as 29·53020 days—today we make it 29·53059 days. Such precision is quite remarkable, and the Maya managed it by a series of equations, including the formula: 405 lunations = 11,959·888 days = 46 tzolkin years of 260 days. They then cross-checked this with other calendric equations.

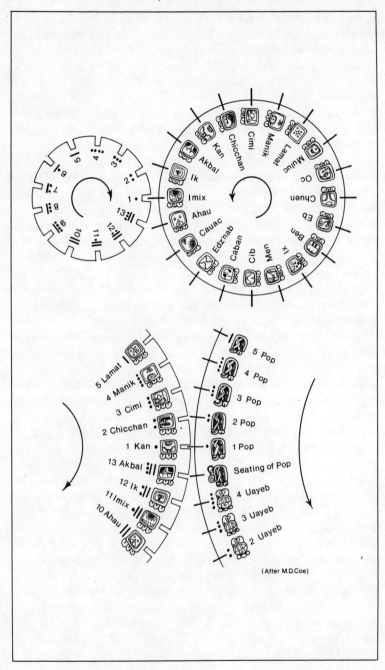

(After M.D.Coe)

Another calendar dealt with the planet Venus (incidentally, the Maya knew, as many ancient peoples did not, that the Morning and the Evening Star were the same planet). They had worked out that the synodical year of Venus averaged about 584 days (it is, in fact, 583·92 days). They therefore calculated a neat equation: 65 Venusian years = 104 *Haab* years of 365 days = 146 *Tzolkin* years of 260 days. Because they were not quite accurate in their estimate of the length of the Venusian synodical year they found error creeping in after long periods of time, and this they corrected by several ingenious devices. The error amounted, in fact, to only one day in more than 6,000 years. (It will be noted, incidentally, that the Venusian cycle is exactly double the cycle which marks the coincidence of the *Haab* and *Tzolkin* years, i.e. 52 *Haab* years and 73 *Tzolkin* years.)

Most of the information about the Mayan Venusian cycle and other astronomical data can be found in the Dresden Codex (so-called because it is kept at Dresden in East Germany), one of the three surviving Mayan books. There is a suggestion that another astronomical table in the Codex refers to the synodic year of Mars, which has 780 days. Others have been thought by some authorities to refer to Mercury and Jupiter. These questions are undecided.

With the help of their calendars, the Mayan priests were able to predict eclipses of the sun and moon, thus enabling the proper rites to be observed and the proper sacrifices to be made, and ensuring that especially susceptible persons, such as pregnant women, stayed hidden indoors till the danger was past.

67 opposite page *Aspects of the Mayan calendars. The top two circles illustrate the* Tzolkin *calendar: the 20 months of the circle on the right interlock with the 13 days of each month, represented by the circle on the left, making a total of 260 days in the* Tzolkin *year. The bottom two diagrams show how the* Tzolkin *calendar on the left interlocks with the* Haab *calendar on the right. The* Haab *calendar has 18 months of 20 days each, with an additional 5 or 5½ special days known as* uayeb, *making a total of 365 days. The two calendars completed their interlocking cycle once every 52* Haab *years (73* Tzolkin *years), thus providing a check for the Maya on the accuracy of their calculations.*

68 *Two pages from the Dresden Codex, one of the three surviving Mayan books. The Codex appears to be chiefly concerned with the rotations of the planet Venus, but two-thirds of the characters have still to be deciphered.*

The Maya Long Count Calendar was based on a year, or *tun*, of 360 days. The table was compiled as follows:

20 *kin* (or days)	= 1 *uinal* (month)
18 *uinal*	= 1 *tun*
20 *tun* (or 7,200 days)	= 1 *katun*
20 *katun* (or 144,000 days)	= 1 *baktun*
20 *baktun* (or 2,880,000 days)	= 1 *piktun*
20 *piktun* (or 57,600,000 days)	= 1 *kalabtun*
20 *kalabtun* (or 1,520,000,000 days)	= 1 *kinchiltun*
20 *kinchiltun* (or 23,040,000,000 days)	= 1 *alautun*

It is hard to imagine what prompted the Maya to carry the tables into these upper projections or, moreover, what use they could have made of them. As a further complexity in interpreting Mayan dates, each day had a name, or rather, two names—one in the *Haab* and one in the *Tzolkin* calendar. There are likewise particular glyphs for the gods presiding over certain days, and time glyphs indicating the katun, baktun and other periods into which a recorded event falls.

THE HIEROGLYPHS

Glyphs were the Mayan form of writing. As can be seen over-leaf, each glyph was approximately square, with rounded corners. Within this outline was a complex design in which parts of the human body, such as jaws, hands and eyes, were often detectable. Other designs, on the other hand, were entirely abstract. There were also often subsidiary designs attached to the main cartouche which seem to be prefixes and affixes and which evidently altered the meaning of the glyph. In some glyphs the bars and dots of numerals can be discerned. The glyphs were arranged in double vertical columns and were to be read from top to bottom and from left to right. Mayan glyph writing was in principle similar to Chinese, each glyph representing a complete word rather than a letter of the alphabet. The glyphs are also reminiscent of Egyptian hieroglyphic writing. But sadly such analogies are of little help in attempting to decipher their meaning.

Bishop de Landa believed that the Mayan glyphs were an alphabetical script. With the aid of a Mayan interpreter, therefore, he wrote down the glyph or sign for the letters of the alphabet he knew. Although valuable, de Landa's decipher-ment has not, however, supplied the key needed to read Mayan writing. It is thought that one of the difficulties may have arisen from the interpreter misunderstanding what was wanted and providing the names of the letters rather than their sounds. Thus, a stranger endeavouring to learn the English alphabet might run into difficulties if, on pointing to the letter 'h', he was told that was 'aitch'. The information given would be correct but would not help him at all when he tried to match the sound of the spoken language to the written word. More fundamentally, however, de Landa was setting himself an impossible task, for although there are some alphabetic elements in the Mayan script there are many more that are ideographic and pictographic.

In his monumental work *Maya Hieroglyphic Writing* the British archaeologist Eric S. Thompson examined the problems of Mayan script in great detail. A few examples will serve to show what some of them are. In Yucatec Mayan, the word *xoc* has two meanings: the verb 'to count' and a mythological fish. So in a glyph which incorporates the idea of counting we find the idea represented by the head of a fish. In Mayan mythology the *moan* bird (a kind of horned owl) is a creature which, from its home in the sky, helps to send rain to the earth. Since the rainy season was the most important part of the year for the maize-dependent Maya, the glyph for 'tun' (year) in the Haab calendar showed the head of the moan bird. The first month of the Haab year was called pop, which was also the Mayan name for a mat of plaited rushes. So a mat appears in the glyph for 'pop'. (This also contains a subsidiary idea, for as the mat or pop on which the chief sat was a symbol of authority, so it was appropriate that the first month of the year should be similarly distinguished.)

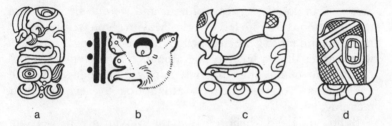

a   b   c   d

69 *Some examples of Mayan hieroglyphics: (a) 'xoc'; (b) a 'Moan' bird; (c) 'tun'; (d) 'pop'. Read the text above and then see if you can make out what they represent.*

In order even to start trying to decipher the Mayan glyphs, therefore, the scholar needs to have an intimate knowledge of Mayan mythology and folklore. The task is not made easier by the Mayan passion for filling in every available space with designs. Some of the glyphs are elaborate to the point of complete confusion, and it is difficult to determine which are the essential parts of the design. While the problem of reading the Mayan books and inscriptions bristles with difficulties, however, it cannot be deemed impossible. The fact that dates and other chronological records, which comprise nearly one-half of the available material, can be understood engenders confidence that sooner or later the rest too will yield. Scholars in many parts of the world are working at it, and at the time of writing the Russians think they may have found the key. We have the advantage that Mayan is not a dead language. Yucatec Mayan is probably very similar to the Mayan of Classic times, bearing the same relationship to it, in fact, as perhaps modern English does to the English of the Middle Ages. It is therefore largely a matter of matching the glyphs to the spoken word.

What are we likely to learn about the Maya when we can read the glyphs? The answer may be somewhat disappointing. Undoubtedly we shall learn more of their history, particularly from the inscriptions. A date appears on almost every important building erected by the Maya, and when we can read the accompanying glyphs we shall obviously acquire much additional information. Important advances have already been made. It has been shown for example that, of a number of stelae from Piedras Negras which have been intensively studied, each represents the events of a single reign. There are glyphs depicting the king's birth, accession and marriages, the births of his children, his victories and his eventual death, all accompanied by dates. From glyphs in friezes at Yaxchilan the American scholar, Tatiana Proskouriakoff, has compiled a history of the dynasty of 'Jaguar' kings who ruled there in the eighth century A.D.

The decipherment of Mayan writing will probably also reveal a great deal more about Mayan religious beliefs and mythology, on which we are already fairly well informed, and doubtless there will be many prophecies. Hopefully the glyphs may also include poems and other forms of literature. Mayan traditions from the years after the conquest say that some of the books destroyed by the Spaniards contained medical lore, but although information about the knowledge the Maya had of herbal medicine would be interesting, what we know so far about their mumbo-jumbo of omens and divination does not provide grounds for optimism that the Maya really had a great deal of worthwhile medical knowledge.

The Mayan priests based many of their prophecies on the idea that history is cyclic, and that what has been will be again. They believed that the world had passed through four great cycles, each measuring almost exactly 5,200 years (or 13 baktun). Each had ended with some cataclysm, such as flood or fire. We are now in the fifth cycle, which began in the year 3113 B.C., and they calculated that this would come to an end in the year A.D. 2011; they were sufficiently precise in their estimates even to predict an exact date in that year—24 December.

Just as the cycles repeated themselves, moving inexorably towards their inevitable conclusion, so events within the cycles were likewise repeated. It was therefore argued that if the precise dates of past events were known, when the same conjunction of dates came around again the same events would recur. Thus a well-informed priest could accurately predict forthcoming events. In particular there was a minor cycle of 257 years, which was a manageable period. It was subdivided into 13 katun, of approximately 20 years. As each katun came under the same occult influences as the katun of the same name which had preceded it 257 years earlier, it was likely to produce a similar sequence of events.

Such exactitude in prophesying bred a kind of fatalism. Since a certain sequence of events seemed inevitable, it was futile to try to alter them. As a result, when the last independent Mayan city, Tayasal, was still defying the Spaniards in 1696, a Franciscan priest, Avendano, who had studied the Mayan calendars, visited the town and pointed out to its rulers that, according to the prophecies, their downfall was certain: within a few months the end of the age of the old religion was due, and Christianity would then replace it. His submissions, with which the city's rulers felt unable to argue, undermined their will to resist, and, though beset with doubts and reservations, they allowed the Spaniards in. A parallel example, of course, is the classic one of the last Aztec emperor, Montezuma, who, when Cortes and his Spaniards appeared, hesitated until it was too late because of prophecies that the white god Quetzalcoatl would return that very year from the eastern sea.

There is a curious by-product of this preoccupation with predictions based on the past. In post-conquest Mayan literature it is seldom clear whether the writers are referring to actual history or to forecasts based on long-past events. The books of Chilam Balam, for example, of which parts of 10 or 12 volumes survive, were written in the Mayan language but in European script at various periods between the Spanish conquest and the late eighteenth century, apparently in an attempt to preserve some of the ancient lore of the Maya people. Although extremely valuable, however, the books are riddled with errors, many of which arise from a confusion of actual events with prophecies. (A somewhat similar example is provided by the biblical Book of Daniel which professes to be concerned with events in the distant past of the Babylonian monarchy but is actually a graphic account, fictionalized for reasons of security, of a resistance movement in Palestine some 400 years later—in about 160 B.C.)

9

Art and architecture

The ancient Maya left a wonderful legacy of art and architecture. Although painting was not, perhaps, the chief of the arts at which they excelled, it is more convenient, for the sake of continuity with the previous chapter, to give it priority here. The Maya used painting mainly in their books. The 'paper' employed was made from the inner bark of a fig tree, which was beaten, pounded and stretched to a proper consistency. It was then prepared in long sheets, some 8–12 inches wide and many times as long. These were folded to give pages about 3 or 4 inches wide, and were painted on both sides. The paper was covered with a lime-wash to provide a smooth surface. The paintings in the surviving codices were apparently done with a thin brush, and the dominant colours are red and black, though there is also some green, yellow and brown. In the case of the Dresden Codex, the workmanship is excellent, but the others are less meticulous.

A few more examples of Mayan painting occur on pottery and stone, and even on jade. However, most probably did not survive the ravages of Central America's damp, tropical climate. As a result the superb example of the rooms at Bonampak seems even more of a miracle. There are three of these rooms, which were discovered as recently as 1946. Together they comprise a building 44 feet long by just over 13 feet wide and tapering to a vaulted ceiling 16½ feet above the floor. The walls, including those sloping up towards the ceiling, are covered in rich murals, depicting vivid scenes of Mayan life and in particular some connected with a military campaign or raid. There are scenes of battle, of the subsequent triumph, of prisoners being tortured, of

70 *In the exquisitely painted rooms of Bonampak the ceilings and corbelled walls are covered in murals depicting scenes from the life of a warlike chieftain. Here we see his attendants preparing themselves for a sacrifice.*

dancing accompanied by music, of councils of state, and, by way of contrast, some domestic scenes. It is thought that the whole is a record of some victorious campaign, or perhaps the events of a reign of a warlike chief.

The colours of the Bonampak murals are brilliant, the figures lifelike and the whole work of art remarkably well executed. It brings to mind the Egyptian tomb paintings, except that the figures are less stilted and the art forms less conventionalized. In addition to their artistic excellence, the paintings provide much valuable information about dress, customs and other aspects of Mayan life.

The murals were painted straight on to plaster which was between one and two inches thick. Von Hagen asserts that the plasterer and artist must have worked together, the artist drawing on the cement while it was still wet: 'The whole of the three rooms must have been painted in 48 hours,' he says. Hieroglyphics, so far undeciphered, accompany the paintings and may one day tell us exactly what they depict.

Although Bonampak is the supreme example of Mayan art discovered to date, there are other notable specimens elsewhere, the earliest being at Uaxactun. It is likely that much Mayan sculpture, too, especially the abundant work in bas-relief, was originally painted.

SCULPTURE

The murals of Bonampak are so astonishingly lifelike that Mayan sculptures in general produce a sense of anticlimax. They are conventional, stylistic and often cluttered with overmuch detail, though the workmanship is usually excellent. To appreciate them we need to understand their purpose. Like so much of the ecclesiastical art of medieval Europe, Mayan sculptures were fashioned for the glory of God (in this instance, gods, in the plural). Much of the European art of the period had the additional object of instructing an illiterate people in the stories associated with their faith: the Mayan sculptures, on the other hand, are generally situated in temples or parts of temples to which the public never had access. They were intended for the eyes of the gods alone, or, at the most, the eyes of the gods and a few privileged priests. Most of them are representations of the gods.

One can appreciate that with such a confusing galaxy of gods as

71 *Two examples of Mayan sculpture. The one above comes from the ruins of a court in Copan, the one on the opposite page, in which the elongation of the skull is very pronounced, is from Palenque.*

the Maya possessed, it was important to get the god's details right, so that he could be correctly identified. Mistakes could be costly. A society capable of punishing a dancer for losing rhythm or a musician for sounding a wrong note would have been equally severe on a sculptor who, deliberately or otherwise, made an error in the representation of a god. The knowledge must have had a cramping effect on the artist's style. So we are confronted with rows of stylized figures, pompous in appearance, conventional in posture and clad in symbolical finery, notably headdresses. It is only in subsidiary details, such as the foliage around a god's feet and the animals and birds that play there, that the artist allows his imagination free play. Analogies are

again to be found in the churches of medieval Europe, where assiduous students may find a wealth of exuberant carvings of characters and creatures, both zoological and mythological, on bench ends, choir stalls and gargoyles.

It is worth remembering that the profusion of elaborate Mayan sculpture which has survived, besides much more which has perished, was accomplished with only stone tools. In the earlier periods of Mayan civilization most sculptures are in bas-relief, but later artists also became accustomed to working in high relief and in the round.

Through the centuries there were gradual changes of style, and archaeologists make maximum use of these in tracing the history

72 opposite *The sun-god, from a stela at Palenque dating from about A.D. 700. In contrast to the vivid murals, Mayan sculptures tend to be conventional and overcluttered with detail.*

73 above *Formal Mayan decorative designs on the wall of the palace ruins at Mitla. These elaborate patterns were achieved with only the most primitive of stone tools.*

of the various cities. The earliest bas-reliefs, for example, show figures in very much the same attitude as those on Egyptian tombs, namely, with the face and feet in profile but with the body full-face. Nearly always they look to the left. Gradually the convention becomes more liberal and by the seventh and eighth centuries A.D. Mayan artists seem to have been able to tackle any commission with equal versatility, showing figures either facing or side-face, standing or sitting. A revival of art occurred in the time of the New Empire, under the Itza and their Mexican allies,

74 above left *A beautifully-fashioned vessel, dated A.D. 800–1000, found in the valley of Ulua, Honduras. It is made of calcite, and was probably used as a ritual bowl at sacrifices.*

75 above right *This stone Atlantid figure holds up a table in the ruins of Chichen Itza. It represents a late expression of Mayan art, dating from the tenth century A.D*

but its quality is depreciated by being too flamboyant and crowded with detail. Several new artistic features also appeared, particularly at Chichen Itza from the tenth century A.D. onwards. These include the Chac Mools, the Atlantids, the standard-bearers and a solid type of stone throne or stool adorned with the carved heads of jaguars.

ARCHITECTURE

Mayan sculpture was mostly found in the stone buildings which are in many ways the chief expression of Mayan genius. Mayan architecture evolved from the simple Mayan house, many of which stood on a low platform or dais. Some of the more important buildings in the cities were built on top of a series of platforms, of decreasing size, so that the approach to them was by way of steps. Such an arrangement, pushed to its logical

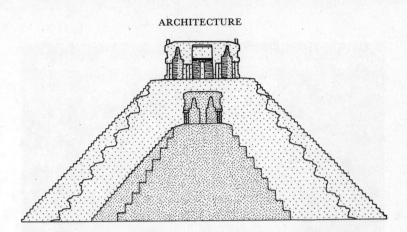

76 *A section through the Castillo at Chichen Itza, illustrating how one pyramid was built on and around an earlier one.*

conclusion, results in a pyramid, truncated at the top. A newly built pyramid would be covered with stucco. The archaeologist Eric S. Thompson was lucky enough to have seen one in more or less its original condition, revealed by stripping off a later pyramid which, in the Mayan tradition, had been constructed around it. He described it as follows:

> The whole surface of the pyramid is covered with a thick layer of light cream stucco, dazzlingly bright, when first excavated, in the clear tropical sunlight. One of the most impressive and touching sights I have ever seen was this pyramid, bathed in the light of a full moon . . . Few white men have seen or will see it in its pristine beauty, for with each rainy season and with the unchecked growth of vegetation more of its stuccoed surface disappears. It can be but a matter of a few years before it is reduced to a shapeless mass . . .
>
> In the flat stuccoed summit were four post-holes, forming a rectangle about 16 feet by 11, evidence that a temple of perishable materials had once crowned the pyramid. Its size, that of an average room, would have permitted ceremonies requiring the presence of six or eight priests.

Sacrificial victims were very often hurled from the summit of pyramids, usually after but sometimes before death. It might be surmised that this was the chief purpose of the pyramids, and so it

77 *A reconstruction of the Temple of the Cross at Palenque, showing the temple building on top of its tiers of steps. The whole surface of the pyramid would be covered with a thick layer of light cream stucco, dazzlingly bright.*

may have been, but in 1952 an exciting discovery was made which disproved the contention that the pyramids were never used for burials. Dr Alberto Ruz Lhuillier, a celebrated Mexican archaeologist, was excavating at Palenque when he noticed in the floor of the Temple of Inscriptions, which stands on the summit of a pyramid 65 feet high, a stone marked by a series of unexplained holes. Managing to lift the stone, he discovered a descending stairway deliberately blocked with rubble. It led, by a devious route, to a room on the same level as the base of the pyramid. Here were five or six skeletons, evidently of sacrificial victims, and beyond that a gigantic stone slab. When this was moved, Lhuillier found himself in the burial chamber of a *halach uinic*, whose skeleton lay, encrusted with jade and jewellery, under a great sarcophagus. It would appear that the burial was made before the pyramid was built and that the latter may therefore have been intended as a memorial to this great man.

The huts of the peasants and the temple pyramids were the two extremes of Mayan architecture. Between them, in style, were

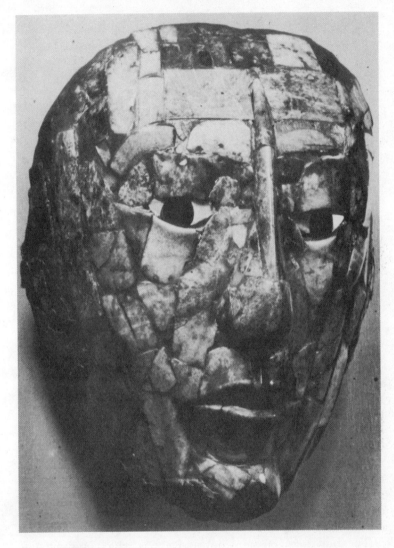

78 *A life-sized mosaic mask in jade, from a funerary crypt in the temple at Palenque. It dates from the late seventh or eighth century A.D.*

79 *The Castillo at Chichen Itza, a particularly well-preserved example of a Mayan pyramid. This is the same building as is shown in the diagram on page 125.*

numerous buildings that were grouped around the temples and the great courtyards that marked the centre of Mayan cities. They are generally termed 'palaces', but their real use is not clear. The rooms are dark and windowless, and often much of the interior is occupied by a raised dais. They would make uncomfortable dwellings and seem better suited to ceremonial purposes. It has therefore been suggested that they were used by men of the higher classes for the lengthy preparations, involving days of fasting and sexual abstinence, for important religious ceremonies.

The buildings, often of impressive size, rise tier upon tier around the plazas, like huge iced cakes. They are chunky, solid and rectangular. The roofs are not quite flat but seldom if ever have a slope of more than twelve inches—just sufficient to allow the rains to drain off. A curious feature of many of them is a central roof crest or comb, a towering, tapering double wall many feet high running along the apex of the roof. Its purpose seems to have been ornamental. In some cities the upper sections

80 *The Maya failed to discover the true arch. Their only method of constructing an arch was by corbelling, illustrated here with a superb example from the Governor's Palace at Uxmal. The large stones are fitted together with remarkable precision.*

of the walls sloped inwards at a modest angle, giving the impression of a mansard roof.

Mayan cities made use of the local stone for their buildings. Most of those in Yucatan are of limestone; some of the highland ones employed sandstone, volcanic rock and even adobe. The western regions, now in the Mexican state of Chiapas, did not have any building stone and so used kiln-baked brick. The cores of the pyramids and of the platforms on which the temples and palaces were built were generally of rubble. In the case of the limestone of Yucatan, this would set as hard as rock. It has been estimated that for one of the pyramids at Tikal about half a million cubic feet of rubble and masonry support three rooms which have a combined floor space of less than 150 square feet. The number of man-hours required for this undertaking must have been colossal, though that was doubtless a factor of which the oligarchy of Tikal took little account.

A curious deficiency on the part of the Maya, parallel with their failure to appreciate the value of the wheel, was their failure to discover the true arch. Their only method of constructing an arch was by corbelling. This involves allowing the stones of two parallel walls to project progressively towards each other until a capstone can eventually be added to complete the arch. It is a principle that requires great care, for any attempt to speed up the process by making the arch too flat brings with it the danger of collapse.

CIVIC BUILDINGS

Other buildings grouped around the central plazas of Mayan cities include the ball courts and certain public buildings, including the equivalent of sauna baths. In the sweat rooms the Mayan client, presumably a member of the aristocracy or perhaps a merchant, sat in a bath of steam created by pouring hot water on stones; then he retired to an adjacent chamber to cool off. Where a city relied on a *cenote* for its water supply, they often lined it with cement or stone. In many instances a city used two (or more) *cenotes*, one for their water, the other as a place of sacrifice.

A feature of Mayan cities, Copan being an outstanding example, are the stelae erected in front of the palaces or temples. Copan has 38 of them, many with an associated altar, or what appears to be an altar, nearby. Some of these stelae have been

81 *Temple buildings at Labna, showing the decorative stonework and the large arch.*

shown to record the events of a single reign, complete with dates.

Copan, one of the largest of the Mayan cities, has 5 major plazas and 16 smaller ones. Tikal is even larger, and its main plaza measures 400 feet by 250 feet. Around these central squares, the Mayan cities sprawled haphazardly. The inner suburbs were perhaps inhabited by the aristocracy, some of whose houses, though probably made of wood, which has perished, had stone floors which have survived. The ordinary citizens lived on their little farms in a wide zone farther out. A Mayan city thus resembled, in some major respects, a modern American one, with its central block of tall buildings and a spacious residential zone encircling it.

Raised and paved causeways led to the central plazas and

linked them with other plazas. Almost certainly they were used for ceremonial processions. They were, however, extended from city to city, to form a road network surpassed in the Americas only by the great road system of the Incas. Mayan roads, called *sache* (which means 'white way'), were constructed on a base of large, roughly-shaped stones, surfaced with limestone chippings or gravel. They were consolidated with the help of large and very heavy stone rollers. They apparently had a standard width of $14\frac{1}{2}$ feet. The early Spanish chroniclers paid tribute to the excellence of the Mayan roads, most of which have, of course, now disappeared, though the course of some of them may be detected from the air. It is strange that this splendid road system should have been created for a nation of pedestrians, who had no vehicles at all.

10

The cities and their fate

The Mayan cities, as cities elsewhere, grew like spring flowers, enjoyed their summer of glory and then either experienced a natural decline into sere old age or were slashed into oblivion. In the following brief summaries of the histories of some of the most important of them it must be remembered that, at the best, our information tends to be sketchy. We see the ruined pyramids and penetrate into the snake-haunted and spider-infested corridors of the adjacent 'palaces'. We tread the jungle-tormented pavements of the great plazas; we decipher the dates on the various buildings and monuments; but we cannot read even the ancient names of most of the cities. We admire the graphic portraiture of chiefs and war leaders but in most instances we can only guess at who they were and what they did.

It must be remembered, too, that the cities belong to long ago. Although in this book we have been insisting that the Maya are not a dead and forgotten race, the period of their Classic splendour is indeed far in the past. The last independent Mayan stronghold, Tayasal, fell in 1697, when William III was on the throne of Britain and when William Penn was establishing the colony of Pennsylvania. Mayapan, the chief city of the last great Mayan state, was destroyed 51 years before Columbus sailed for the New World. The great days of the Classic Period of Mayan civilization coincided with the Dark Ages of Europe, beginning approximately with the fall of the Roman Empire and ending at about the time when Western Europe was being devastated by the Vikings. The early centuries of the Classic Period were coeval with the T'ang dynasty in China, the later ones with the first flowering of the Arab civilization in the Near East.

The cities described in this chapter are arranged in a rough order of chronology. The selection is not perhaps strictly scientific, in that it necessarily falls on those cities of which we have some knowledge; moreover, particularly for the earlier periods, we have inadequate information for gauging their relative importance. There are the ruins of scores, perhaps hundreds, of great cities which the spade of the archaeologist has never touched littering the jungles of Central America. When they have eventually been investigated, not only will our knowledge of the Maya be immeasurably increased but some of our ideas may well have to be revised.

IZAPA

This city lies about 20 miles inland from the Pacific Ocean, on the western side of the Suchiate river which here forms the modern boundary between Mexico and Guatemala. It is a large site, with more than 80 temple mounds. It flourished in very early times, apparently before the development of glyph-writing and the calendar, and is thought by some authorities to represent a link between the early civilization of the Olmecs and that of the Maya proper. The influence of its art style is noticeable in other sites in the Guatemalan and Mexican highlands.

KAMINALJUYU

This city was situated just to the west of modern Guatemala City, which is why we know a great deal about it. As Guatemala City has grown, so its suburbs have encroached on the ancient site, destroying much of it. Even the towering temple mounds, of which there were originally several hundreds, have been de-molished till only a few remain, but rescue digs have provided us with more knowledge of Kaminaljuyu than we possess of most highland Maya sites.

It seems that Kaminaljuyu was flourishing in the Formative Period of Mayan culture, between about 800 and 300 B.C., when it produced a distinctive type of pottery and also some sculpture. It continued to flourish for several centuries more but gradually sank into decline and appears to have been almost abandoned by about A.D. 400.

The name 'Miraflores culture' has been given to this early flowering of the Mayan genius. The numerous mounds which distinguished the site until recent times were platforms on which temples once stood. In the absence of good building stone, they

82 *A beautifully fashioned stone head from the ruins of Kaminaljuyu, one of the oldest Mayan cities of the Guatemalan highlands.*

were constructed mainly of clay and were therefore easy prey for modern bulldozers. The temples which surmounted them were probably of timber, with thatched roofs. Tombs that have been excavated reveal that the rulers who erected the temples lived in considerable luxury. They were buried beneath the temples with a wealth of treasure, much of it in jade. After each interment it seems that a new floor was added, thus increasing the height of the temple pedestal. It is interesting that at this relatively early date temple platforms which were, in effect, truncated pyramids were being associated with burials.

The inhabitants of Kaminaljuyu evolved a system of writing, using glyphs, which has not yet been deciphered but which apparently bears a resemblance to early Mayan. There were among them gifted artists, especially in painted ceramics. Links with the culture of Izapa are many. Early in the fifth century A.D. Kaminaljuyu, or what was left of it, came under the influence of distant Teotihuacan. The town was probably still in existence but sadly deteriorated. The enterprising merchants of Teotihuacan first probed the commercial potential of the Guatemalan highlands and then, recognizing a fruit ripe for the picking, possibly followed up with a military venture. Thereafter, for several hundreds of years (exactly how long is not known), Kaminaljuyu prospered again under a foreign dynasty. The Esperanza culture which is associated with this Mexican influence is typical of Teotihuacan; after a time it also developed some Mayan traits.

Kaminaljuyu was only one of a number of Mayan centres which grew up in the Guatemalan highlands in the Formative Period. Among others are Monte Alto, El Baul, Abaj Takalik and, in what is now El Salvador, Tazumal and Usulutan. El Baul has contributed one of the earliest known inscriptions in the Mayan Long Count—a date corresponding to A.D. 36.

UAXACTUN

Uaxactun was one of the great Mayan cities of the Peten, formerly a thickly populated Mayan region but now one of the emptiest areas on earth. The oldest date deciphered on the site is A.D. 328, but the city was doubtless in existence earlier, and new buildings were still being erected in A.D. 850. The French archaeologist Paul Rivet has estimated that the city at its height had a population of some 50,000.

Uaxactun has produced one of the earliest examples of Mayan stonework—a temple dating from the second century A.D., which has been preserved because, in Mayan style, it was enclosed by a later pyramid. It consisted of a series of platforms, the topmost one having originally been occupied by a temple or shrine of timber, with a thatched roof. The similarity between this and the temples of Kaminaljuyu is evident; like them, it had been used for burials, with a new floor added after each interment. Uaxactun also has some of the oldest Mayan sculptures and frescoes, the latter being the finest examples of Mayan painting known until the painted rooms of Bonampak were discovered in 1946.

The latest recorded date at Uaxactun is towards the end of the ninth century A.D. Soon afterwards the city seems to have been abandoned, in the mysterious way characteristic of Mayan history. Thompson suggests that it may have been only the central area of the city which thus became derelict, perhaps through a popular uprising which drove out the priests and nobles. Burials on the old sites at somewhat later dates indicate that the neighbourhood was still populated by people among whom the old traditions survived.

TIKAL

Perhaps the greatest of all Mayan cities in the Classic Period, Tikal is situated in the jungles of the Peten, 11 miles south of Uaxactun. It appears to have been founded at about the same time and is, naturally, closely linked with Uaxactun. It has been suggested that until about A.D. 435, when a period of expansion began, Mayan civilization in the lowlands was confined to an area of about 30 miles radius around these two cities.

Tikal covers a huge area, only the centre of which has been properly surveyed. Its great plaza is on an artificially levelled plateau of limestone lying between two ravines, which were dammed by the Maya to form water reservoirs; the dams also served as roads or causeways. Tikal has eight enormous temple pyramids and scores of lesser but still impressive buildings. Some of the pyramids rise to a height of over 200 feet. There are also more than 80 massive stelae and scores of altars. Hieroglyphics are carved everywhere, many of them on wooden lintels over the doorways to the pyramids.

From the type of sculpture characterizing the fifth century A.D.

at Tikal, some authorities surmise that the influence of Teotihuacan was strong here as at Kaminaljuyu. Whether the impact came by trade, conquest or colonization is not certain. That was not, however, the beginning of Tikal, for evidence of habitation dates from 600 B.C. Nor is anything known of the end of Tikal. The latest date so far discovered on inscriptions there is A.D. 869. When the Spaniards arrived, nearly 700 years later, the site was nothing but a series of spectacular ruins in the jungle.

YAXCHILAN

This was one of the cities marking the period of expansion from the Tikal–Uaxactun region early in the sixth century A.D. The earliest date recorded on inscriptions here is 514. The city lay on the north (now the Mexican) side of the large Usumacinta river, on the edge of the Peten. It extended for a mile or two along the terraced river bank and had eight large, though not particularly high, temple pyramids and many other fine buildings. The archaeologist Dr Michael Coe regarded the numerous stone lintels of Yaxchilan, covered with hieroglyphics, as 'perhaps the most complete documents we have for the temporal dynasties which ran the ancient Mayan centres.' The site has not yet been extensively explored by archaeologists, however.

Yaxchilan had a particularly warlike dynasty in the eighth century, and its end seems to have come shortly afterwards, in the ninth.

BONAMPAK

This was not a major city and is included only because of its now world-famous murals. The paintings illustrate a war or raid carried out by the chief of Bonampak about the year A.D. 800; possibly, since it has been suggested that Bonampak was a dependency of Yaxchilan, he was a member of the Yaxchilan dynasty referred to above.

PIEDRAS NEGRAS

Another city of the Classic Period on the Usumacinta river, about 25 miles downstream from Yaxchilan. The name, which is Spanish, refers to the black stones which occur in the area and is not the one by which the Mayan city was known. The earliest recorded date is 534, the latest A.D. 810. The site has much fine sculpture, chiefly on lintels and stelae, and other features include several sweat-baths. Links with Yaxchilan were evidently close.

83 *This temple pyramid at Tikal, one of the greatest Mayan cities of the Classic Period, still remains to be excavated.*

84 *Two views of the Mayan city of Palenque, which flourished A.D. 317–987:* above *the Temple of Inscriptions, on the opposite page the Old Palace. Palenque lies in hilly country, with magnificent views of the forest-clad Usumacinta plain below.*

PALENQUE

Situated on a jungle tributary of the Usumacinta, some 60 miles north-west of Piedras Negras, Palenque was one of the earliest cities to be archaeologically investigated. The amount of attention it has received may account in part for its high reputation, but the city is indeed one of the finest of all the Mayan centres. 'It was there,' says Paul Rivet, 'that Mayan sculptural genius reached its climax, the artists having at their disposal a calcareous stone as hard and fine as lithographic stone. It was there that stucco was handled with the greatest mastery.'

Palenque is in hilly country, affording a magnificent view of the forest-clad Usumacinta plain below. Its name, like that of Piedras Negras, is Spanish (meaning 'palisade'), the Mayan name being unknown. The city seems to have been founded later than most of those in the region, the earliest deciphered date being A.D. 642. As the latest is only 783, the period of Palenque's superb florescence appears to have been short.

XICALANGO

As the crow flies, a journey of just over 70 miles from Palenque would bring one to Cerrillos on the coast, thought to be the site of the ancient port of Xicalango. The Mayan cities so far considered are now vast, abandoned ruins in the jungle or forest. Xicalango has no such pretentious ruins, yet it endured much longer than the cities of the interior and was there, still flourishing, when Cortes arrived.

Xicalango was a thriving market, on the very edge of Mayan territory. Its very name is said to have meant 'the place where the language changes'. It was situated not on the open sea but on the shores of the extensive Laguna de Terminos, in a district noted for its salt production. Its trade was mainly by sea, with the Mayan ships coasting around the Yucatan peninsula to the ports of northern Honduras. Obsidian, jade, copal, quetzal feathers, cocoa-beans, flints, emeralds and other products were, however, brought down from the highlands over a well-made network of roads.

Little is known of Xicalango's early history, but it is recorded that the folk-hero Quetzalcoatl took refuge here in about A.D. 987.

QUIRIGUA

This city marks the southern limits of Mayan territory, as Xicalango does the north-western. Trading ships from Xicalango rounded Yucatan and anchored in the port of Nito (now Livingston, in Guatemala). From there traders would make their way inland some 40 or 50 miles to Quirigua, on the Motagua river.

Quirigua is not one of the most imposing of Mayan cities. It has few stone buildings and no temple pyramids, but what it does possess are some exceptionally fine and massive sandstone stelae, one of which stands nearly 25 feet high. Their dates indicate that Quirigua flourished from about A.D. 692–810. It is at Quirigua that an inscription giving a Long Count date of 90 million years has been found.

COPAN

This southernmost of all the great Mayan cities of the Classic Period lies about 30 miles south of Quirigua. The dates suggest that it was flourishing from A.D. 460–801. It is situated in the valley of a lovely tributary of the Motagua river, and, as it lies at an altitude of over 2,000 feet, enjoys an ideal climate.

Its ruins are a spectacular complex of temples, plazas (five large ones and many smaller), an acropolis and a series of connecting stairways of impressive dimensions. The most imposing of all, the Stairway of Hieroglyphics, has 63 treads, each carved with glyphs, of which there are calculated to be at least 2,500. The stairway was dedicated in the year A.D. 756. Other inscriptions indicate that nine years later (in 765) scholar-priests from most parts of the Mayan territory met at Copan for a conference called to correct certain errors that had crept into the calendar. Copan, it seems, was a recognized centre for astronomical studies.

From the point of view of art, the craftsmanship exhibited by the hieroglyphics is exquisite. All around is an exuberance of sculptures, of gods, animals, birds, humans and mythological

85 *Quirigua, near the southern limits of Maya territory, is not one of the most imposing of Mayan cities, but it possesses some exceptionally fine sandstone stelae. This one, carved with the dates and events of a king's reign, stands nearly 25 feet high.*

creatures. There are 38 splendid stelae, with numerous associated altars, and a number of pyramids, the highest of which rises 130 feet above its base. Its ball court, which has been restored, is one of the finest known.

CALAKMUL

This city, deep in the heart of Campeche state in Mexico, was a principal Mayan city in Classic times. Its inscribed dates indicate a florescence from A.D. 514–810. Its 103 stelae comprise the highest total of any Mayan city.

CHICHEN ITZA

Unlike the other cities so far considered, Chichen Itza enjoyed two periods of glory. After its abandonment in Classic times it achieved a resurrection at the end of the tenth century and thereafter, for 300 years or so, flourished even more brilliantly than in its previous summer.

It seems to have been founded about the middle of the fifth century A.D., on a flat site near two large *cenotes*, but little is known

86 *In the splendid city of Chichen Itza the Pyramid of Kukulkan occupies a prominent position. This is where the feathered serpent god, known alternatively as Kukulkan or Quetzalcoatl, was worshipped. In the foreground is the courtyard of the Temple of the Warriors.*

of its early history beyond the fact that it was abandoned towards the end of the seventh century.

Then, according to some authorities, in the second half of the tenth century a civil war in the Mexican kingdom of the Toltecs, whose capital was Tula, 50 miles north of Mexico City, drove a large number of defeated Toltecs into exile. Under a leader named Quetzalcoatl (in Toltec—Kukulcan in Mayan), they sailed across the Gulf of Mexico and landed on the Yucatan coast. There they found themselves in a kind of vacuum, as a result of the inexplicable abandonment of many of the old Mayan cities. They settled in Chichen Itza, rebuilt it and made it their chief capital.

The narrative is, however, confused with the story of the Itza, who were a Mayan tribe formerly living in the area. They seemed to have left their home at Chichen Itza in earlier centuries and to have settled for a time around the coastal city of Chakanputun. Apparently they made common cause with the Toltecs, and their united forces are frequently referred to as the Itza.

Archaeology will doubtless throw further light on the subject. At any rate, the brilliant civilization that developed at Chichen Itza in the centuries following A.D. 987 was certainly in part Mexican. Mexican gods were worshipped, particularly the feathered serpent god who represented the deified hero, Quetzalcoatl-Kukulcan; new styles of architecture, closely related to those of distant Tula, were evolved; and the city was clearly under the domination of an alien military caste, in which the knightly orders of the Jaguar and the Eagle achieved prominence.

In our own age Chichen Itza has become celebrated for its sacred *cenote*. For centuries this was a place of pilgrimage. Generations of Maya threw costly presents and even human sacrifices into it, and its dredging by modern archaeologists has yielded a rich harvest of Mayan valuables.

In 1194 a civil war broke out between Mayapan and Chichen Itza in which the former city was victorious. The ruling class of Chichen Itza, known in the chronicles as the Itza, were expelled, though the city was not entirely abandoned by the ordinary people. No new buildings were erected, and the existing ones were neglected. It seems that some of the Itza rulers were taken as hostages to Mayapan, but others wandered off through Yucatan, eventually coming to rest on the shores of remote Lake Peten

87 *The courtyard of the Temple of the Warriors at Chichen Itza. The columns depict scenes from the reigns of warrior kings.*

146

88 *This well-preserved range of buildings at Uxmal was named the
Nunnery by the Spaniards, who assumed that it housed the equivalent of
vestal virgins. The notion was almost certainly mistaken.*

Itza, where they founded the city of Tayasal, the last independent Mayan state of Middle America.

UXMAL

All the cities of the later epochs of Mayan civilization were in the
north of Yucatan. Chichen Itza is situated in the centre of the
peninsula, about 60 miles from the north coast. Uxmal is about
80 miles to the south-west, and 40 miles inland from the west
coast.

Uxmal, now partially restored though with only its central
areas investigated, is one of the most imposing Mayan cities. It
spreads itself spaciously over a vast area and is dominated by two
great pyramids. Around these extend immense groups of buildings, dignified by such names as the Palace of the Governor, the
House of the Turtles and the Nunnery. The last-named was
assumed by the Spanish conquerors to have been the apartments
of the equivalent of Vestal Virgins, but almost certainly they

89 top *Stone decoration from the walls of the Palace of the Governor at Uxmal. The building was probably the city's administrative centre.*

90 above *Another view in Uxmal shows a fine example of the Mayan corbelled arch.*

91 *An excavated pyramid at Labna, one of the chief Mayan cities of Yucatan.*

were mistaken. The House of the Governor may, however, have been correctly identified, for it seems to have been an administrative centre. It covers five acres and is reputed to be the largest and finest building ever erected in pre-Columbian America.

KABAH

Kabah is one of a group of 20 or more cities which apparently flourished at the same time as Uxmal, making this region one of the most densely populated of ancient Mayadom. An identified date here reads A.D. 879. The city is situated some 13 miles southeast of Uxmal.

LABNA, SAYIL, XKALUMKIN, OXKINTOK, XKICHMOOL

These are other cities of the Uxmal-Kabah group, many of which possess massive and magnificent buildings and courtyards. They are linked by an effective road system.

The colonial and modern city of Merida occupies the site of the Mayan city of Tiho.

92 *Even the lesser Mayan cities such as Sayil, depicted here, possessed much magnificent architecture.*

DZIBILCHALTUN

An extensive city, of which very little was known until it was investigated by archaeologists a few years ago. It covers at least 18 square miles and has more than 21,000 temples and other sites. Although it apparently flourished at the same period as Uxmal and the other Yucatan cities it is built on very ancient foundations; it is said that the site was continuously occupied from about 1000 B.C. Dzibilchaltun lies due north of Merida and is about 15 miles from the sea.

IZAMAL

Izamal lies about 40 miles due east of Merida and is about the same distance from Chichen Itza. Of it an early Spanish writer (in 1633) recorded that it was a place of pilgrimage accessible by 'four roads running out to the four cardinal points which reached to all ends of the land, Tabasco, Guatemala, Chiapas, so that today in many parts may be seen vestiges of these roads.' Izamal was, in fact, the home of two important Mayan gods, Kinich-kakmo, a manifestation of the sun-god who has here one of the largest pyramids in Central America, and Itzamna. It flourished in the age of Chichen Itza and Mayapan, featuring in a Helen-of-Troy-like episode which precipitated the war that ruined Chichen Itza, but its history extended over many earlier centuries.

TULUM

This was a comparatively small but important seaport on the east coast of Yucatan. Unlike most Mayan cities it was surrounded by a defensive wall, which it probably owed to its overlords, the rulers of Mayapan. It was founded, however, at a much earlier date, having certainly been in existence in the sixth century A.D. The city wall is a massive affair, up to 20 feet thick and rising to a height of 15 or 20 feet, with only five narrow entrances, admitting just one person at a time. Unlike most Mayan cities Tulum was still populated during the Spanish era.

COBA

This was an important centre, 30 miles inland, for which Tulum was the port. It was the hub of an impressive road system. The best preserved road links the city with Yaxuna, 62 miles away (and a few miles south of Chichen Itza), and to do this it has to cross numerous swamps which it does by means of causeways. Coba is thought to have been founded in the fourth century A.D. and was probably a place of pilgrimage in early times. It is now ruinous. A road links it with Xelha, another port just north of Tulum.

MAYAPAN

Mayapan dominated the Mayan cities of Yucatan for several centuries until it was sacked in 1441. The Mayan chronicles state that around the year A.D. 987 the three cities, Chichen Itza, Uxmal and Mayapan, formed a league which controlled all northern Yucatan for about 200 years. Then civil war resulted in the destruction of Chichen Itza and the establishment of a centralized state at Mayapan.

From the beginning Mayapan was apparently a city of the Mexican invaders, by whatever name they were known. It is unequivocally a military stronghold. The site is barren rock and would never have been chosen by a government interested in its agricultural possibilities. The city was defended by a formidable wall, 10–12 feet thick and up to 12 feet high. The wall was $5\frac{1}{2}$ miles long and enclosed an area of some $2\frac{1}{2}$ square miles. Inside this there were, according to a recent estimate, some 3,500 houses, indicating a population of perhaps 20,000. There were also suburbs outside the wall.

Mayapan was not, however, a well-planned city along European lines. The buildings were arranged haphazardly, without streets. Archaeologists consider its architecture degenerate compared with the brilliance of the earlier cities of the Peten and of Uxmal and Chichen Itza. Thompson has pointed out that 'the best masonry is found in the residences of the nobility, not in the temples. Beautifully dressed stone robbed from the site which preceded Mayapan is re-used with considerable frequency in private homes, but crude stonework of the Mayapan period is good enough for many of the temples.' On the other hand, there seems to have been an increase in the incidence of human sacrifice. The impression left is of a city dominated by robber barons and *nouveaux-riches* merchants, battening on tribute pouring in from the surrounding region. Apparently one of the measures by which the rulers of Mayapan ensured the subordination of their neighbours was a system of hostages, with important members of the 'royal' families of the tributary cities forced to live permanently in Mayapan. Eventually a rebellion was engineered by a Mexican Mayan family, the Xiu, who seem to have been the same as the one associated with Uxmal. It was successful. The rulers of Mayapan were slaughtered, the city sacked and looted. The date usually given for this event is A.D. 1441, but it may have been a little later.

Mayapan is situated in central northern Yucatan, some 30 miles north-east of Uxmal and about the same distance southeast of Merida.

TAYASAL

When in or about A.D. 1194 the Itza were driven out of Chichen Itza, the survivors wandered southwards through Yucatan and the Peten until they finally came to rest at Tayasal, on an island in Lake Peten Itza. There they built a new city, which was visited and spared by Cortes and which continued to maintain its independence and what was left of Mayan civilization until 1697. Its site is now mostly submerged under the Guatemalan town of Flores.

Aftermath

After the fall of Mayapan in or about 1441, Yucatan disintegrated into a medley of little city-states engaged almost permanently in internecine war. The situation resembled that of
Britain in the Dark Ages, after the fall of the Roman Empire.
The confusion was aggravated by a hurricane which devastated
the country in 1464 and by an epidemic (nature unknown) which
caused much mortality in 1480.

The first Spaniards arrived on the coasts of Yucatan in 1511,
and another epidemic, of smallpox, which swept the peninsula in
1515–16 was certainly introduced by them. Exploratory expeditions by the Spaniards landed in Yucatan in 1517, 1518 and,
led by Cortes himself, in 1519. However, since they found little
gold there, they bypassed Yucatan for the time being.

In 1524–5 Cortes with a small army, including Mayan and
other Indian allies, made one of the great marches of history from
Tuzantepetl, on the Gulf of Mexico, across the wilds of Tabasco,
Yucatan and the Peten to subdue a revolt in Honduras. His route
took him through some of the most desolate and least populated
parts of Central America, and it has been suggested that his
Indian guides made sure that this was so. The official conquest of
Yucatan was not begun until 1527–8, when the task was
undertaken by Francisco de Montejo, with a basic force of 380
men and 57 horses.

Montejo had a more difficult assignment than Cortes had had
in Mexico or Pizarro in Peru. There was no central government
with which he could treat after a swift campaign. Each city had
to be taken separately. The Maya, by this time aware of the
reputation of the Spaniards and of what they had done in

93 *A detail from 'The Conquest of America', a painting by Jan Mostaert (1470–1555). In their battle with the Spaniards the Maya were handicapped by their traditional view of war, which they conceived as an episode of limited duration, after which life resumed much as before. The Spaniards, on the other hand, were bent on a ruthless war of conquest.*

Mexico, avoided pitched battles but proved themselves adept at guerilla warfare. They chased Montejo out of his first base, the city of Xelha; then out of his next choice, Chetumal, farther down the coast, on the borders of what is now Belize. One of the leaders of the Maya was a renegade Spaniard named Guerrero, who was finally killed by a chance shot at Ulua, in northern Honduras. The war continued with little change of fortune after his death, until by 1535 the Maya were everywhere victorious and the Spanish had been expelled from Yucatan. At this juncture Montejo, a disappointed and weary man, retired in favour of his son. The assault was resumed in 1542, when the Spaniards achieved sufficient success to found the city of Merida, on the site of the old Mayan town of Tiho. The house which the younger Montejo built in 1549 still stands by the central plaza of Merida.

The war became more ferocious, and the Maya suffered from two handicaps. One was that they were hopelessly divided. As in Mexico, certain tribes saw the Spaniards as allies to help them pay off old scores against their neighbours—a fatal concept, as they later realized. The other handicap was that the Maya considered war as an episode of limited duration. Though fierce and bloodthirsty while it lasted, it came to an end, after which life went on much as before until the next engagement. The Spaniards had other ideas. They were fighting a war of subjugation, of which the ultimate aim was the enslavement of a population. Montejo, in return for a large sum of money raised by pawning his wife's jewels, had received from the King of Spain a grant of 1,000 square miles of territory in Yucatan. His followers divided it between themselves according to the usual custom of Spanish conquistadores, allocating to each landholder a grant of serfs—Maya sold into perpetual servitude.

With the conquerors came the Spanish Church, eager to save the souls of the poor Indians by all their well-tried methods of persuasion. One of the earliest missionaries was Bishop Diego de Landa who, after equipping himself with some knowledge of the Mayan language, undertook a walking journey through his diocese. Meeting with comparatively little success in his attempts at peaceful conversion, he adopted more drastic methods, including the wholesale destruction of idols, shrines and Mayan literature. He was so successful that, as we have seen, only three Mayan books survived. A zealous, humourless prelate, he was equally severe with his Spanish flock, ordering floggings for failure to attend Mass on Sundays. Paradoxically, he has proved to be one of our main sources of information on Mayan life at the time of the conquest and earlier, for, recalled to Spain to account for the excesses of his period of office, he spent his time while awaiting examination writing a *History of Yucatan*. Even more valuable was the study he prepared of the Mayan language, which has provided a key to at least the partial decipherment of the glyphs.

So, with the violent disruption of their old way of life, the Maya became virtually the property of white masters on the haciendas which occupied great areas of Yucatan. They were not willing peons and from time to time rose in revolt. Serious uprisings occurred in 1847, 1860 and 1910. Meanwhile, although they ostensibly became good Catholics and attended Mass regularly, the old religion remained alive and vigorous. It has now become so merged with the Catholic faith that it is difficult to unravel the separate threads.

In the highlands a similar pattern of events occurred. The Maya of Guatemala were left alone until Mexico had been conquered. Then in 1523 Pedro de Alvarado was despatched southwards to subdue the mountain tribes, the chief of which was the Quiche. Inevitably, the Indians were divided. Another tribe, the Cakchiquel, saw an opportunity to get their own back on their old enemies, the Quiche. Treachery and betrayal abounded, and de Alvarado distinguished himself by his ruthlessness and cruelty. The highland cities of Utatlan and Iximche fell in 1524; Zaculeu and Mixco Viejo in 1525. The Spaniards built new capital cities—Santiago de los Caballeros (destroyed by earthquake, flood and mud in 1541), and another Santiago, known as Antigua Guatemala, destroyed by earthquakes in 1717 and 1773 but now flourishing again.

Thus was Guatemala integrated into the Spanish Empire, the turbulent history of which it shared in the subsequent centuries past the end of colonial times and into the era of the independent republics. Today there are still millions of Mayan Indians living as they have always done in mountain, forest and jungle villages, descendants of the Maya of long ago, and one day perhaps inheritors of their great artistic and cultural genius.

94 *With the conquering Spaniards came the Spanish Church, eager to save the souls of the poor Indians. At Cholula in Mexico, although not in Mayan territory, the Spanish church of Los Remedios, perched on the top of a huge Toltec pyramid (one of the largest pyramids in the world) typifies the triumph of the European way.*

The rediscovery of the Maya

This book departs from the usual pattern of books on the Maya in that it concentrates on the Maya themselves rather than on the authorities who have 'discovered' them. In the absence of much written history it is, however, impossible to ignore those who have painstakingly pieced together such facts as we have.

One of the earliest writers on the Maya was the Spanish Bishop Diego de Landa, who compiled his volume in the 1560s. In his later years, regretting his over-zealous destruction of manuscripts, he spent much time collecting relics of the Mayan civilization and talking with high-ranking and educated Maya. His Mayan alphabet has proved less useful than he could have hoped, for the Mayan hieroglyphics are not entirely alphabetical, but it is still of considerable value to scholars. His book was lost to the world for 300 years, but in the mid-nineteenth century a copy was found in a Madrid library by a young priest Etienne Brasseur de Bourbourg. Thereafter de Bourbourg kept an eye open for other Mayan literature and one day found an old Mayan–Spanish dictionary in a Mexican market. His discoveries proved of immense value when scientific interest in the Mayan civilization began at last to awaken towards the end of the nineteenth century.

Several Spanish writers set down accounts of what they saw in Central America in the sixteenth century, and a few books compiled from Mayan sources were written in Spanish script. Of these latter, the most important are *The Book of Chilam Balam*, *The Annals of the Cakchiquels*, and the *Popul Vuh*. Chilam Balam is supposed to have been a Mayan sage who prophesied the coming of the Spaniards, and the book was compiled from various sources. Some of it is reliable history, but much of the information it contains is based on the Mayan practice of projecting the events of one katun into another, on the theory that history repeats itself. As a result there are great difficulties in disentangling the two. The Cakchiquel were one of the chief Mayan nations of the Guatemalan highlands at the time of the Spanish conquest. They threw in their lot with the Spaniards to revenge themselves over their neighbours, the Quiche, but their fortress Iximche was quickly occupied by de Alvarado. The *Popul Vuh* is the sacred book of the Quiche Maya. It relates the Mayan myths about the creation of the world, the origin of their race and the nature of the gods, but gives much incidental information about Mayan history, geography and customs. It was written down in Spanish script in about 1550, and is alleged to have been copied direct from a Mayan painted book. Translations into English of all three books are now available.

The Mayan cities mouldered in the jungles and forests, forgotten and unnoticed for more than 200 years after the Spanish conquest. Towards the end of the eighteenth century, in response to rumours, a Captain Antonio del Rio was sent, with a troop of soldiers, to investigate a lost city buried deep in the jungles of Chiapas. He discovered Palenque. Having struggled back to 'civilization' del Rio wrote a book about it, *Descriptions of the Ruins of an Ancient City*, and presented a report to the King of Spain, who was sufficiently interested to order the preservation of any antiquities found on the site.

His book was later read by Jean Frederic Waldeck, a self-styled Count who, after an adventurous career which included accompanying Napoleon on his Egyptian campaign, made his way to Yucatan when already in his sixties and became an archaeologist. During the two years he was there he compiled a large album of diagrams and drawings of Palenque, which would have been much more valuable if he had been able to resist the temptation of 'improving' on what he saw. Nevertheless, he contributed to the growing interest in Mayan matters. Another early Victorian, Lord Kingsborough, decided that the Maya and the Aztecs and their neighbours were the ten lost tribes of Israel and from 1830–48 published a series of enormous volumes entitled *Antiquities of Mexico*. He rescued many ancient records from oblivion and deserved a better fate than death in a debtor's prison, where he had been incarcerated for failure to meet his printer's bill.

In 1839 one of the great explorers of Mayan country, the American John Lloyd Stephens, appeared on the scene. He was the American consul in Guatemala and was fired with enthusiasm by reports of the lost cities of the jungle. With his friend, the talented artist Frederick Catherwood, he embarked in 1839 on his first expedition to the interior. After many hardships, not the least being torture by the mosquitoes and other abundant insect life of tropical Central America, they found themselves amid the ruins of Copan. After an argument with a local farmer, Stephens bought the entire site of the ancient city for 50 dollars! Unlike Waldeck, Catherwood was a meticulously accurate artist. He drew what he saw, and when in 1841 Stephens's book, illustrated by Catherwood's drawings, was published, the world was at last made aware of the wealth of lost art lying buried in the jungles of Middle America. Recently the story of the two explorers has been written as a book, *Search for the Maya*, by Victor von Hagen (1973).

The effect of Stephens's books (there were two volumes, the first of which ran through 12 editions in nine months) was to create a genuine interest in Mayan archaeology. Until his time, what little was known of the buried cities had been the subject of the wildest speculation, in which Atlantis, Egypt, the lost Israelites and many others figured widely. Stephens and Catherwood were both levelheaded men, not given to romancing, and their conviction that the ancestors of the Mayan Indians still living in the region had built the cities brought an element of sober sanity to the affair. Among the readers of Stephens's books was Alfred Maudslay, an English archaeologist who retraced Stephens's route to see for himself whether the author had been exaggerating. Finding that he had not, Maudslay returned to the forests time and again, bringing back with him vast quantities of plaster from Mayan buildings and moulds of Mayan carvings (moulds made from pulped newspapers, which he carried by the ton for that purpose). His collection was housed in the British Museum, where it still is, and created enormous interest. Maudslay, who was knighted for his achievements, also wrote four volumes of notes about his discoveries.

Other pioneers of Mayan exploration included Teobert Maler, an Austrian who for a number of years after 1867 wandered through the Central American jungles, taking excellent photographs of the ruins he found there. In Europe Ernst

95 *Two drawings by Frederick Catherwood from John Lloyd Stephens's book* Incidents of Travel in Central America, *1841 : on the left an overgrown ruin at Palenque, on the right the front view of a stela in Copan. Stephens and Catherwood were among the first to explore the Mayan ruins, and their work aroused considerable interest in the lost cities buried beneath the jungle.*

Förstemann, librarian at Dresden, made a detailed study of the Dresden Codex and recognized the calculations that referred to the planet Venus.

It was now the turn of scientific organizations in Europe and America to show interest. One of the first in the field was the Peabody Museum of Archaeology and Ethnology, of Harvard University, who between 1892 and 1915 sent 20 expeditions to the Maya lands. The Carnegie Institute of Washington, the University of Pennsylvania, the British Museum, the Mexican Instituto Nacionale de Antropologia e Historia, the Chicago Natural History Museum have all made their contributions. And the work still goes on, in every country that now has a stake in the ancient Maya area. In recent years important excavations have been undertaken by the National Geographic Society, Washington. In 1964 Mexico opened its magnificent National Museum of Anthropology in Mexico City. Belize, which is advised on archaeology by Dr David Prendergast of the Royal Ontario Museum, insists that all Mayan remains are government pro-

perty. The other Central American republics likewise try to exercise some control over their archaeological sites, but the problems are vast, and determined looters still get away with art treasures and sell them to museums in other countries.

Among the best of modern writers on the Maya is Dr Eric S. Thompson who, under the auspices of the Carnegie Institute of Washington, has spent many years studying the subject and has made many expeditions to Maya territory. Dr Michael D. Coe, who has published a number of books on early Central American civilizations, is Professor of Anthropology at Yale University and has led many excavations in Mexico, Belize and Guatemala. Among other books quoted in this volume, *Maya Cities*, by Paul Rivet, who is the founder of the French Musée de l'Homme, has the distinction of offering coloured reproductions of the marvellous wall-paintings of Bonampak. Victor von Hagen is a popular writer on the ancient civilizations of America.

In the past few decades it has become increasingly frequent for students, often those engaged in the preparation of a thesis, to spend a year or two living with a remote community in order to record their customs and traditions. Several Mayan communities have been investigated in this fashion. Large books packed with detail have been the result, and the information thus compiled has been useful in helping to fill in the background to the lost Mayan civilization.

While it might be an exaggeration to say that the study of the Maya is still in its infancy, it is true that we are yet in the fresh morning of discovery. High noon still lies well ahead. There are more sites to be investigated than have yet been disturbed by the archaeologist's spade. Every year brings new discoveries. And in museums and libraries scholars are still wrestling with the problems of deciphering Mayan hieroglyphics. It was only recently that Miss Tatiana Proskouriakoff, of the Carnegie Institution, a leading Mayan scholar, established that the stelae which are a prominent feature of Mayan architecture each record the events of a single reign. And a Russian expert on inscriptions, Yuri Knorosov, is working hard on the hieroglyphics, to which he is convinced he has the key.

Perhaps it is not too much to hope that one day the Maya themselves will again produce learned men who may help us to a better understanding of the nature and achievements of their lost civilization.

96 *The British archaeologist Sir Alfred Maudslay and his team
excavating the ruins of Palenque at the end of the nineteenth century.
Maudslay brought back enormous quantities of plaster casts and paper
moulds of Mayan carvings, which are housed in the British Museum in
London.*

Appendix

Nothing in archaeology, and particularly in the archaeology of Middle America, is static. The archaeologist's spade is increasingly active on Maya sites. Scholars in both America and Europe are devoting long hours to the formidable problem of deciphering the Maya hieroglyphics. Each new discovery adds to our knowledge of the ancient Maya or causes us to modify our former ideas.

Since the bulk of this book was written, the results of many years of excavation at Tikal, where work is still continuing in what is now a Guatemalan National Park, have been published. Apart from an enormous mass of information about the impressive central areas of the city, the investigations produced evidence that makes it necessary for us to revise some of the previous conceptions about the everyday life of the Maya. They showed that an area of some 50 square miles around the central plazas was densely occupied by family compounds, seldom more than 500 yards apart.

Such a density of population precludes the idea of a slash-and-burn system of husbandry. It is now thought that each compound consisted of houses, buildings and a surrounding plot of intensively cultivated gardens. Though doubtless maize was grown, it must have taken its place in a crop rotation which probably included a number of root crops and also ramon trees, which yield an edible fruit, the bread-nut.

Ralph Whitlock
April 1976

Glossary

Ah Kin A high priest
Ah men A minor soothsayer or prayermaker
Al holpop An officer of local militia
At atanzahob A professional marriage-broker or matchmaker
Atl-atl A spear-throwing device
Atole A gruel of maize-meal in water, sweetened with honey
Bacab A class of important gods
Balche A kind of wine
Batab A powerful local official
Cenote A natural waterhole formed by the collapse of a limestone
 cave roof
Chac An elder who assisted at ceremonies and sacrifices; also a
 name of the rain-god
Chiccan A god or spirit, who often took the form of a giant water-
 snake
Chicle The juice of the sapodilla tree, used in the making of
 chewing-gum
Chilan A soothsayer or medium
Copal Incense made from the resin of the copal tree
Haab One of the Mayan calendars, corresponding most closely
 to ours
Halach Uinic 'The chief of men', a leader or king
Huipil A dress
Kub A garment worn by women
Manta A square of cloth, used as a cloak or blanket
Moan An owl
Nacom A military commander
Pati A cloak

Pok-a-tok A Mayan ball-game
Pop A mat of plaited rushes; also the first month of the year
Sache A Mayan road
Tortilla A flat, unsweetened pancake made from maize
Tzolkin One of the Mayan calendars
Uayeb Unlucky days in the year
Valapohov A plant, the leaves of which were chewed to quench thirst

NOTE ON THE PRONUNCIATION OF MAYAN NAMES

Note on the pronunciation of Mayan names
  x is pronounced *sh*.
  ch is as in English.
  u before a vowel is pronounced *w*.
  c is always hard.
The accent usually falls on the last syllable of a word. The Mayan language also contains numerous guttural or glottal sounds, often represented in English script by commas and dots.

Bibliography

Maya Cities, by Paul Rivet (Elek, 1960)
World of the Maya, by Victor von Hagen (Signet, 1960)
Maya History & Religion, by J. Eric S. Thompson (University of Oklahoma, 1970)
The Rise & Fall of Maya Civilization, by J. Eric S. Thompson (Norman, 1954)
Maya Hieroglyphic Writing, by J. Eric S. Thompson (Norman, 1960)
Maya Archaeologist, by J. Eric S. Thompson (Norman, 1963)
The Maya, by Michael D. Coe (Penguin, 1966)
In the Eyes of the Ancestors, by June Nash (Yale, 1970)
Search for the Maya, by Victor von Hagen (Saxon House, 1973)
Zinacantan, by Evon Z. Vogt (Harvard University Press, 1969)
The Two Crosses of Todos Santos (Princeton University Press, 1969)
Discovering Man's Past in the Americas, by George E. Stuart (National Geographic Society, 1969)
Handbook of Middle American Indians, by E. W. Andrews (1965)
National Geographic Magazine (October, 1968, pp. 492–521; January, 1969, pp. 141–50; January, 1972, pp. 124–46; November, 1974, pp. 660–89; December, 1975, pp. 729–99)

Index